Christopher Wood

KETTLE'S YARD, UNIVERSITY OF CAMBRIDGE

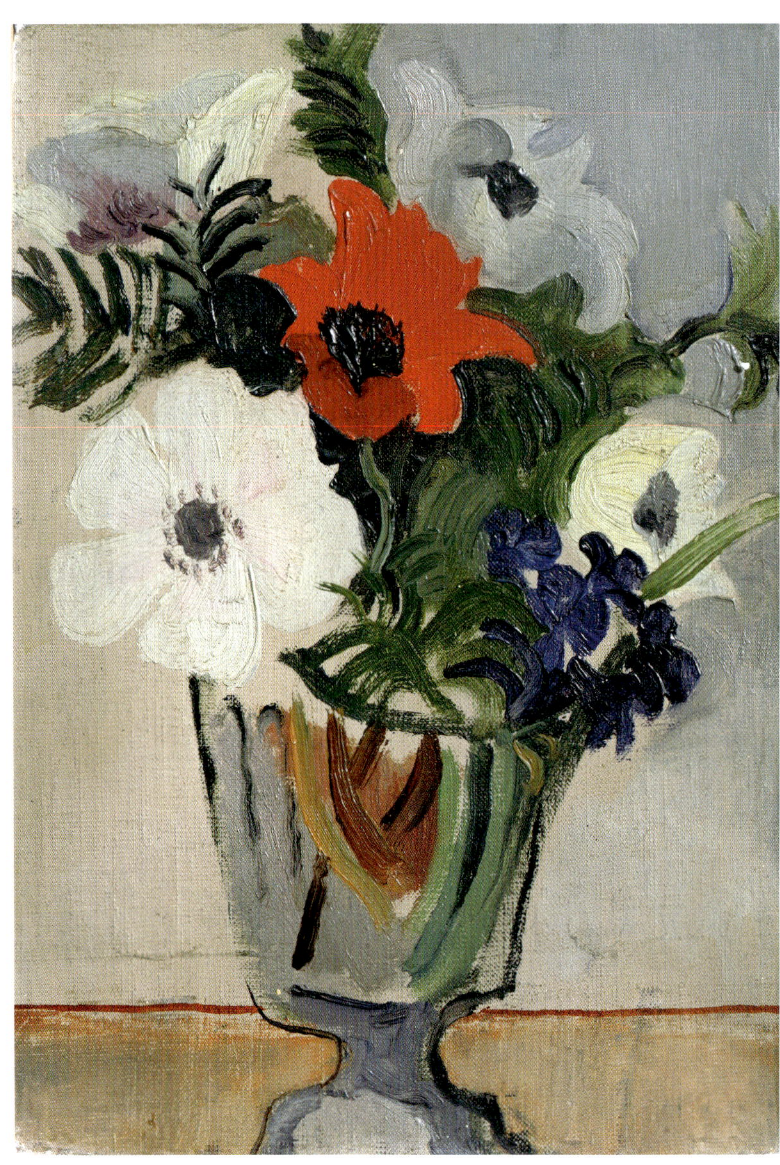

CONTENTS

inside cover:
Christopher Wood with the maquette for ***Luna Park***, photograph by Peter North, 1930

left: ***Flowers***, 1928. Oil on canvas, 214 x 150 mm

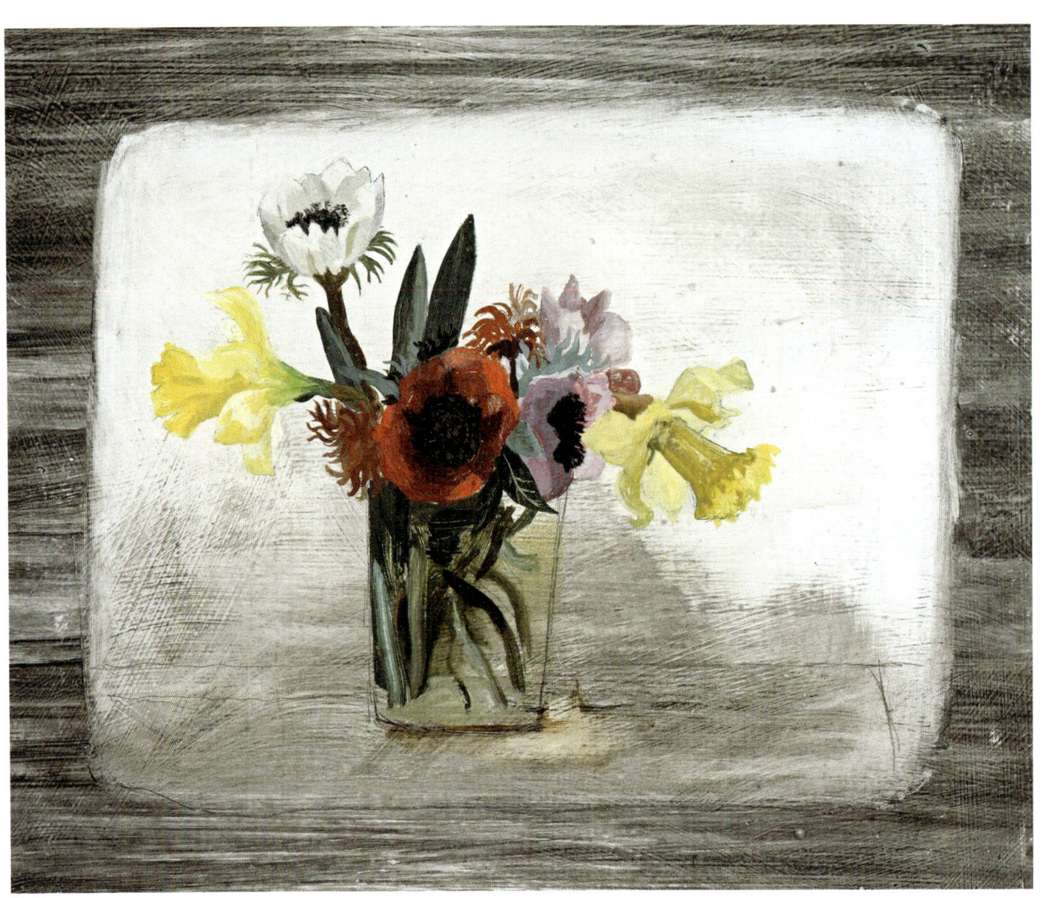

Flowers, 1930. Oil on canvas, 330 x 400 mm

PREFACE

This publication examines the life and work of the British artist Christopher Wood (1901-1930) through the collection at Kettle's Yard. It is the third in a series of new books seeking to examine those artists Kettle's Yard's creator Jim Ede was closest to and who are also best represented in the collection.

It coincides with an exhibition of works by Christopher Wood focusing on the collection that Jim Ede built. Thanks to the generosity of the University of Essex, the exhibition also includes four works that Ede gave to the fledgling university as part of a major gift to seed a new art collection in 1964. The exhibition also includes *La Ville-Close, Concarneau, Brittany* (1930), which was painted during Wood's last and most important period of activity in Brittany and is now part of another University of Cambridge Museum collection, at the Fitzwilliam Museum. Together these works reveal an ambitious and precocious talent, one of the few British artists in the early twentieth century who embraced some of the most innovative European ideas while preserving in his work a distinctive English identity.

The preparation of the exhibition and publication would not have been possible without the tireless work of Jane Morgans, Research Assistant. We are grateful to Claire Daunton, Frances Spalding, Elisabeth Swan and Mary Adams, also Anthony Hepworth, Jessica Kenny and Nigel Cochrane at the University of Essex, and our colleagues at the Fitzwilliam Museum and University of Cambridge Museums. This publication and the exhibition have also benefited from the support of Arts Council England through the University of Cambridge Museums Connecting Collections programme.

As part of the University of Cambridge, we pursue and promote new research through our exhibitions and publications. Through our visual arts, music and public programmes, we reach over 70,000 people a year. None of this would be possible without the vital, ongoing support of our funders and supporters. Our sincere thanks are due to Arts Council England, the Higher Education Funding Council, The Heritage Lottery Fund, The Friends of Kettle's Yard, Cambridge City Council and many individual donors.

Elizabeth Fisher, Curator
Andrew Nairne, Director

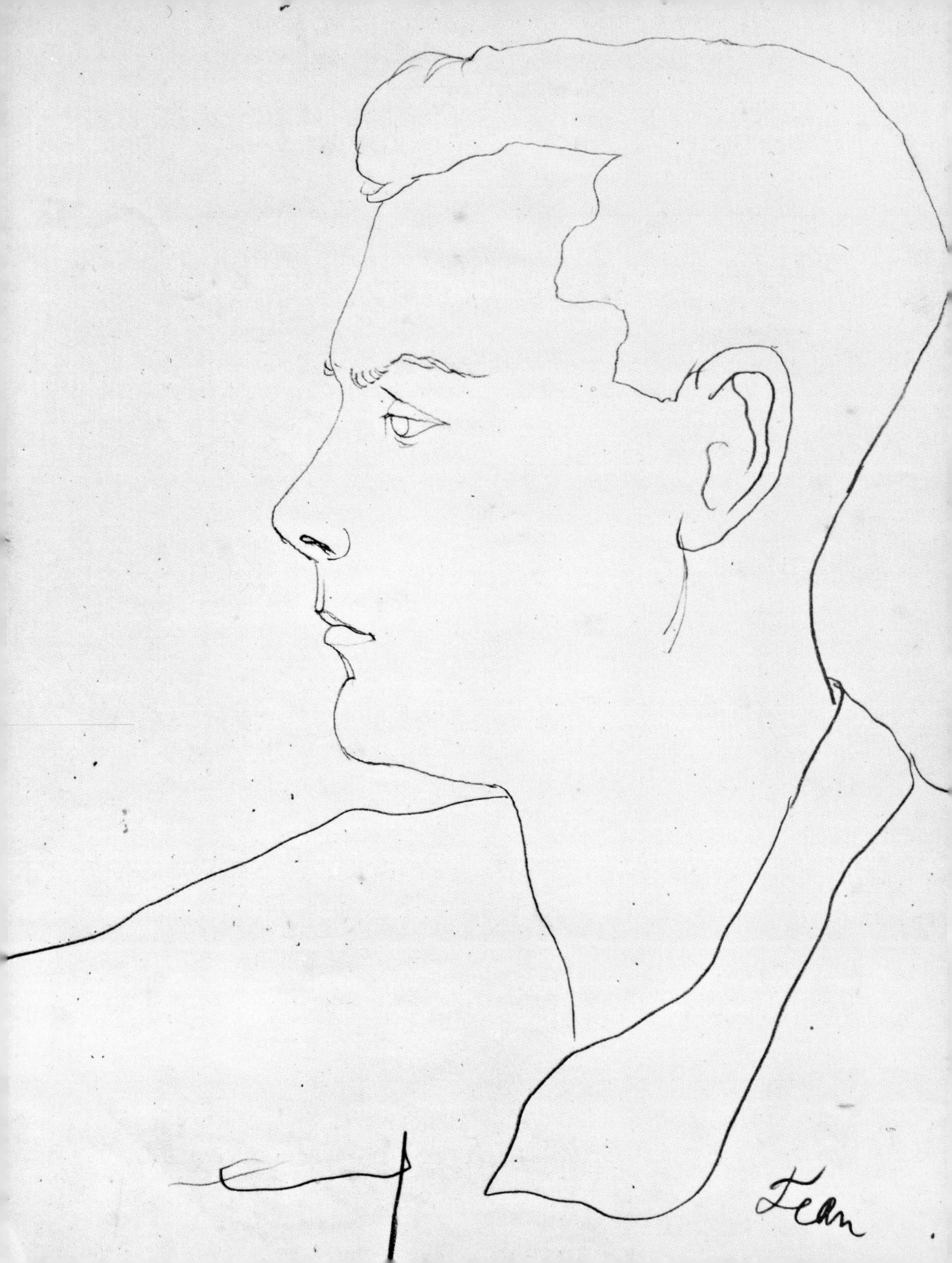
Jean

CHRISTOPHER WOOD at KETTLE'S YARD

Elizabeth Fisher

Kettle's Yard holds the largest public collection of works by the British artist Christopher Wood. This came about largely as a result of the unique relationship that developed between the artist and the founder of Kettle's Yard, Jim Ede. They shared an interest in the artistic developments in continental Europe and both moved freely between London and Paris throughout the Twenties. 'Kit', as Wood was known to family and friends, made Paris his home for much of the decade; between the years of 1924 and 1938, Jim made several trips a year to Paris on National Gallery business, and was able to maintain close, regular contact with artists at the forefront of the avant-garde in Paris. Both recognised the significance of the artistic and cultural changes underway in Paris, and both were frustrated by Britain's isolationist 'slowness' to acknowledge the revolutionary artistic ideas blowing across the Channel. Ede struggled to persuade his superiors at the National Gallery (then an adjunct of the Tate Gallery) to take Picasso, Matisse, Cézanne and others seriously. Wood was one of the few British artists to recognise and respond to the new landscape of modernism.

Jim Ede left 25 works at Kettle's Yard, taking one or two works with him to Edinburgh when he left in 1973. In putting together a careful selection of works for Kettle's Yard, Ede must have been acutely aware that he was creating the largest public collection of the artist's work. Wood's evolving style can be traced through paintings and drawings representing key stages in the artist's development: his pet themes, key relationships, subjects and places – from the flowers Winifred Nicholson would send to him in Paris so that he could paint them, to the maritime scenes of Cornwall and Brittany – are all covered.

Although he was meticulous with his visitor books, Ede's record-keeping when it came to the collection was patchy. There is little information to confirm how the works came to Kettle's Yard. Twenty-one works were listed in the 1966

left: Drawing of Christopher Wood by Jean Cocteau, undated

inventory as having come directly from the artist or artist's estate. He purchased *Self Portrait* from the artist in 1927, and Wood gave Jim *Landscape at Vence (Little White House)* in 1928. Ben Nicholson gave Ede a drawing made in St Ives, most likely made during the summer Wood and the Nicholsons spent together in Cornwall; John Gielgud owned another work by Wood, *Brighton*, which came into Jim's hands before he gave it to Essex. One or two further works have come as gifts since the Edes left Kettle's Yard. It seems likely that the majority of works came into Jim's possession in the process of settling the artist's estate in the early Thirties.

However, we know that in the late Thirties, Jim owned at least 32 works by Kit Wood. The catalogue of the 1938 memorial exhibition of Christopher Wood at the New Burlington Galleries, which Jim was instrumental in arranging, listed an additional 7 works loaned by Ede which are no longer in the collection. Some beloved works, Jim and Helen took with them to Edinburgh when they left Kettle's Yard. Jim gave at least two works, *Young Girl* and *Church and Market, Brittany*, away to owners whose families have subsequently sold these paintings on. Ede's reasons for giving the works away were usually straightforward; they went to homes where they would be loved and cared for as well as they would be in his keeping. Jim's gifts were sometimes pragmatic decisions; in 1938, the Edes left the country to live first in Tangiers, and later at Les Charlottières in the Loire Valley in France. Although they took a number of favourite artworks, including several pieces by Kit Wood, they couldn't take everything. Pictures of White Stone, the house Jim designed and had built in Tangiers, show *Boy with Cat* and *The New Boat, Tréboul* amongst familiar items of furniture. At Les Charlottières, *Le Phare* took pride of place above the fireplace, and fabrics designed by Ben Nicholson draped over the easy chairs. The Edes lived in Tangiers between 1936 and 1950, during which time they met the American singer Libby Holman, a fellow Tangiers resident, who persuaded Ede to part with *Boy with Cat* because the subject of the portrait, Jean Bourgoint, bore a striking resemblance to Holman's late son who had died tragically in a mountaineering accident. Ede sold the work to Holman on the understanding that it would eventually pass back to Kettle's Yard, and so it did in 1974.

Ede's most significant gift, of over 20 artworks to the University of Essex in 1964, included three works by Wood: a lively painting of St Ives harbour, and two characterful drawings of French sailors and some classical-looking nudes frolicking on a beach. Shortly after *Boy with Cat* returned to Kettle's Yard in 1974, Jim gave Essex another, major work: the portrait of Jean's sister, *Mlle Bourgoint*. That year he wrote "there should be a Kettle's Yard in every university".

As he had done with Wallis and Gaudier-Brzeska, Ede played a key role in establishing Wood's reputation as a significant artist. He facilitated loans from the artist's mother, Clare Wood to exhibitions at the Whitworth Art Gallery in Manchester and the Stedelijk Museum in Amsterdam among others, and helped to disseminate Wood's works to public and private collections across Europe, particularly after the artist's death. Ede's habit was to help his artist friends in whatever way he could, using his connections to promote their works, and introducing collectors, gallerists and institutions in the UK and Europe to their work. It was through the purchase of works from friends like Ben Nicholson before they had established careers and were short of money that Jim's own collection began. Perhaps in recognition of his generosity, many artists, including Kit Wood, also gave Jim works.

Ben Nicholson introduced Jim and Kit Wood in 1926, and they quickly became fast and loyal friends. Correspondence and diary entries show they were in regular contact between 1927 and 1930, and often asked after one another via the Nicholsons. But Ede's appreciation of Wood, his efforts on behalf of the artist, and the scope of his collection of works by Wood grew significantly after the artist's death.

Ede's unpublished autobiography, which is written, somewhat awkwardly, in the third person, offers some insight into the reasons for Wood's significance for Jim. His memoirs reveal the personal, even sentimental connection with the individual that grounded his appreciation of certain artists' work. Simply put, Jim valued people first, and art second. This is a value that is still tangible in Kettle's Yard, in it's domestic intimacy – the invitation to sit down and engender a physical relationship with the artworks, and the role of conversation in shaping visitors' experience of the house. He wrote:

> "In asking what had most enriched him he would have put people first, and in this he would have included acts manifested through them … Among Jim Ede's friends he would select a few who contributed outstandingly to his education. From painters Ben and Winifred

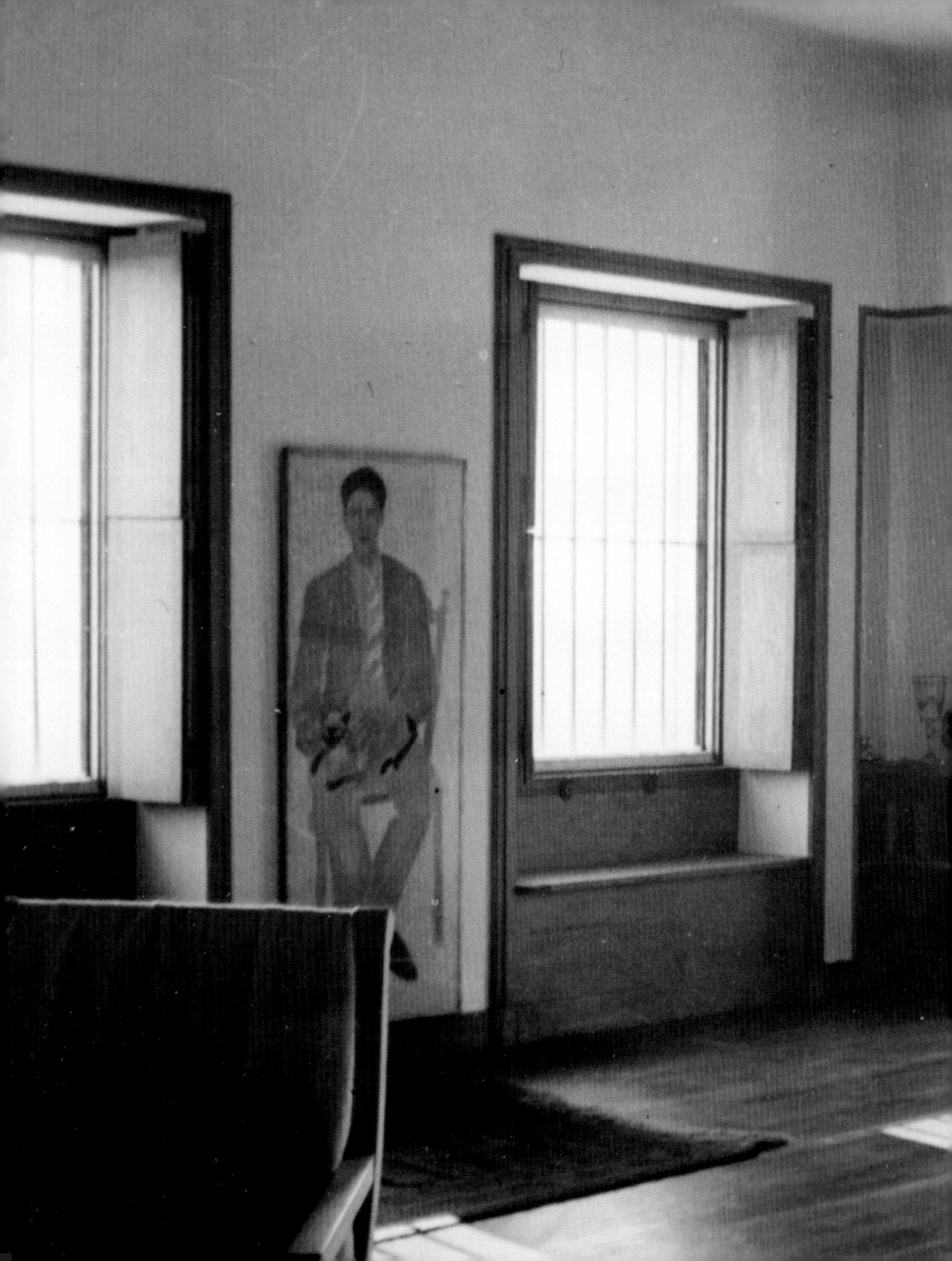

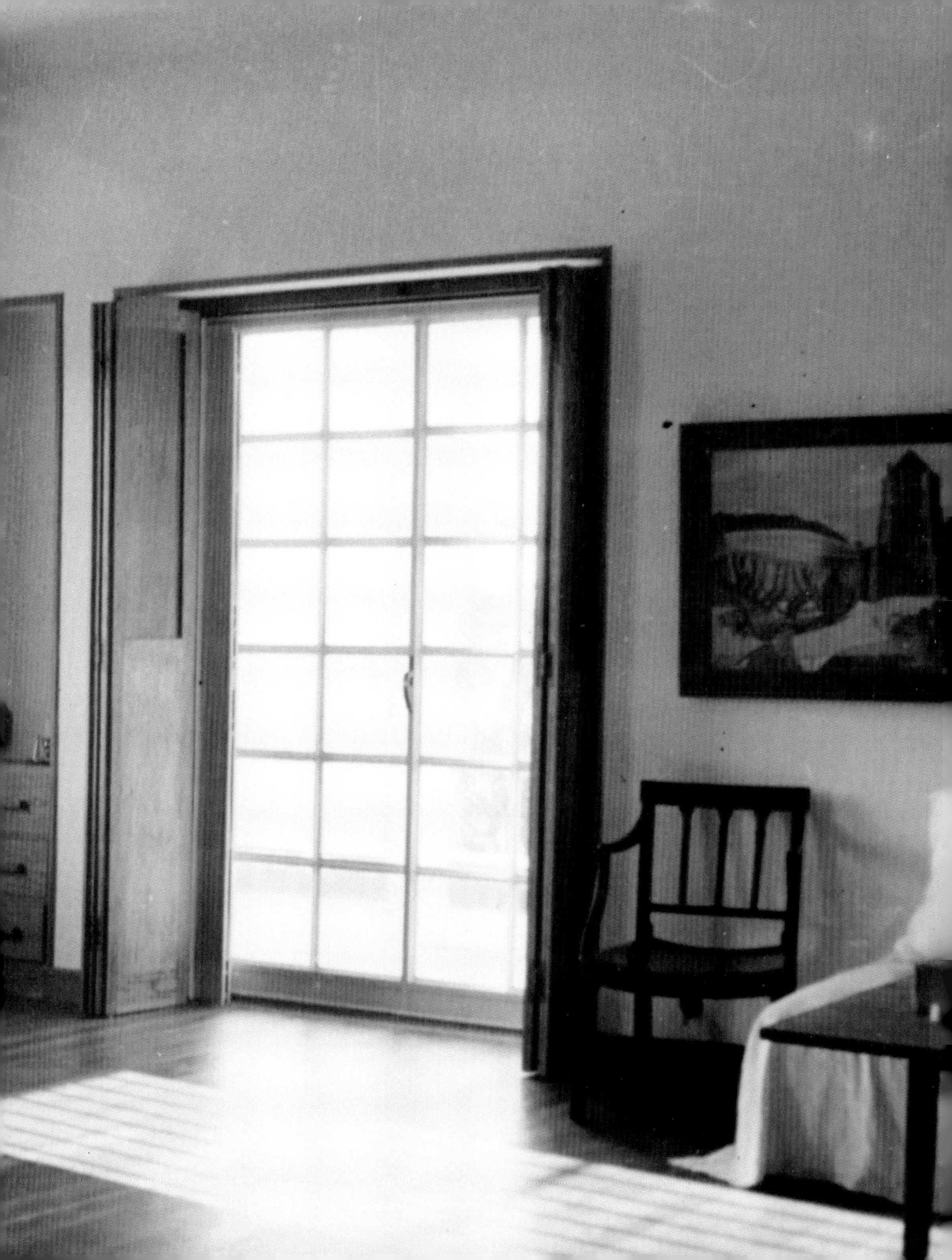

> Nicholson, Christopher Wood and David Jones; he has written of them all, but of their work rather than of their personal stimulation of friendship."

Of Christopher Wood specifically, Ede writes:

> "Christopher Wood influenced Jim more in his death than in his life, for though they were friends, it was only after his death that Jim felt a real intimacy. It was then, for various reasons Jim had a great deal to do with his work and with his way of living, and through him gained considerable clarity of perspective in regard to contemporary painters. Jim learnt from him the direct contact of enjoyment, a simple contact, spontaneous and easy, which became a touchstone in the world of what has often been called naïve painting. This direct expression from nature into paint kept being renewed for Jim and Helen and they found his colour of vision everywhere ...."
>
> "... From Christopher Wood Jim also learnt that things in his paintings, which while he was alive had seemed unfinished and careless, now that they had become unalterable by death, took on a meaning of their own, because of his special style and individual contribution. This happened too with people, some foible which while it could be rectified was a constant irritant, in death became a dear memory."

When Wood died, Ede went, with the artist's mother and Ben Nicholson, to look through the artist's last works at 3 Minton Place. Ede began protracted negotiations on behalf of Clare Wood with Lucy Wertheim, a dealer and recent supporter of Wood who had paid the artist a sizeable advance in May 1930 to enable him to make work for an exhibition in her gallery that autumn. The negotiations soured, enough for Ede to write to Ben Nicholson after a trip to Paris (where he met with Frosca Munster, Alphonse Kahn and Tony Gandarillas among others) at the end of 1930: "I have come home to a terrific row – found a note from my Director accusing me of God knows what dishonourable treatment

previous: White Stone, the Ede's house near Tangiers

right: Les Charlottières, France

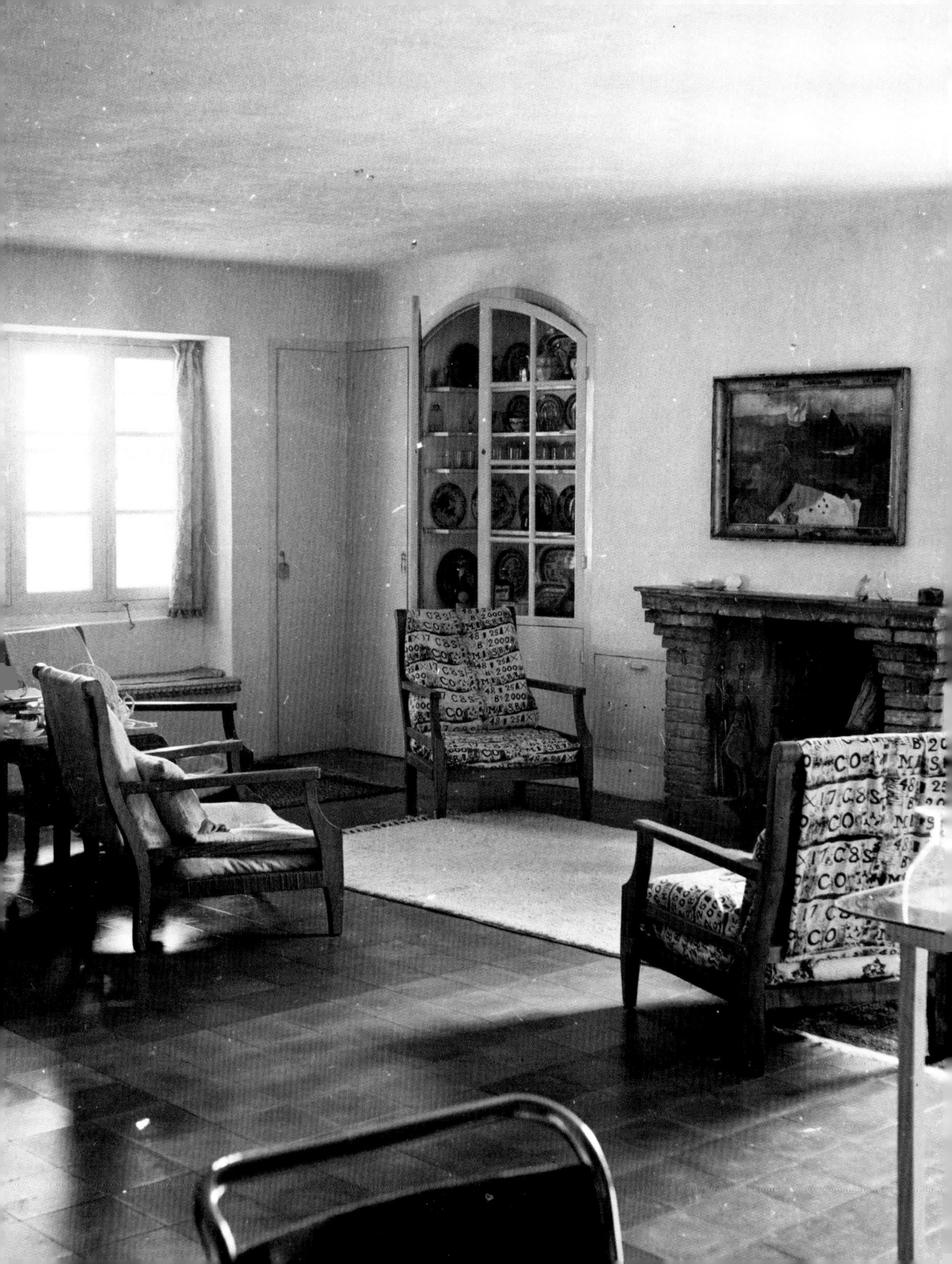

of Mrs Wertheim." Ede already had a difficult relationship with his Director and obviously felt that Mrs Wertheim had misrepresented his efforts in order to exert some pressure over the settling of Wood's affairs. He continues: "Mrs W. evidently still thinks she ought to have those marked pictures and that I have done her out of them. Did I tell you that the Mem. Exhibition was off. She's to have a one man show of her own things and we are to have a Mem Ex where we please and when we please. Perhaps Lefevre Galleries in 1932 – what do you think."

Ede organised the memorial exhibition of Wood's work with the Lefevre Gallery in 1932. According to Virginia Button, a second 'Exhibition of Complete Works by Christopher Wood' organised by the Redfern Gallery at the New Burlington Galleries, Burlington Gardens, in 1938 attracted 50,000 visitors over just one month. A staggering figure in itself for a relatively unknown artist, it is even more startling in comparison to the 15,000 visitors who went to see Picasso's *Guernica* (1937) when it was shown at the Whitechapel Art Gallery earlier in 1938. A vindication of Wood's achievements, it was also telling indictment of the British public's lingering reluctance to embrace the more radical politics and art from across the Channel.

Instead, it was Wood's life and personality that struck a deep chord in the public imagination, while his work offered a more palatable view of the less overtly political artistic developments on the continent. In 1938, with the prospect of a second war in Europe looming, memories of a lost generation of young men were still painful. It was not much of a leap for writers like Eric Newton and fellow artist John Piper to cast Wood, like his contemporary Rupert Brooke and the Romantic poet before them John Keats, as one of England's brilliant but doomed 'golden lads'. This resonated strongly with Ede, who bore his own scars from first hand experience in the trenches.

There were other, wider cultural shifts afoot as a result of the collective trauma of First World War. As Button notes, Wood also represented a particular kind of young manhood that emerged with the generation born between 1900-10. In rejection of their fathers' values which had driven a generation of young men to war, they celebrated fantasy over reality and youth and beauty over maturity. Wood's innocence, combined with the risqué aspects of his lifestyle amongst the beau monde, made him "quintessentially of his time."*

Artistically, there were also powerful role models emerging, and Wood chose both the hero of Picasso and the tortured genius of Van Gogh. Wood aspired to achieve the expressive impact of Van Gogh, and his late work, like Van Gogh's, offers a window into the interior emotional life of the artist. Deliberately or not, this linked Wood to another tragic narrative which held currency at the time: that of the pioneering artist as martyr to his vocation. For all of these reasons beside their friendship, Wood became a key figure in Ede's imagination.

Ede's collection was largely formed during the Twenties and Thirties, when he worked at the National Gallery and was immersed in the London art world. The interwar period was a peculiar moment for twentieth century art. The social, political, and cultural atmosphere across Europe was electric. Ideologues were vying for the social consciousness and economic forces were wreaking havoc across Europe and the USA. Kettle's Yard grew out of an aesthetic vision forged in this context.

Of primary importance to both Jim and Kit was the integrity of direct experience, unimpeded by stylistic affectations or aesthetic conventions. This was the quality they both admired so much in Alfred Wallis: a timelessness in his very brushstrokes, in which art and life were fused. By the time he reached Tréboul in 1930, Kit's pursuit of this artistic vision consumed him. He was isolated and inspired in an ancient place that seemed to turn its back on the rest of the world, a place suspended in time. This made him one of Ede's artistic touchstones. Kettle's Yard is itself a place set slightly apart from the rest of the world, a place in which the pace and hubbub of modern life is drowned out by an immersive aesthetic experience.

As Ede's autobiographical reflections acknowledge, the tragic impact of Wood's death when he had just begun to realise his artistic ambition, and the personal loss that his friendship meant to Jim, permanently coloured his view of the work. Wood represents an artist whose life story is inseparable from the development of his work. He also embodied a formative moment in British art, entangled in questions of individual and national identity. "We find in Christopher Wood one of those who mark an epoch in the art history of a nation", Ede wrote in a lecture on British art for American audiences in 1936. For Ede, a seasoned connoisseur of modern art, the drama and timbre of Wood's life took on a significance in death that softened his criticisms of weaknesses in Wood's work, and allowed him to see them as precious aspects of a unique artistic voice. In this lies one of the most important lessons of Ede's aesthetic vision: that of the humanity of art.

*Button, Virginia, *Christopher Wood,* London: Tate Publishing, 2003, p.20

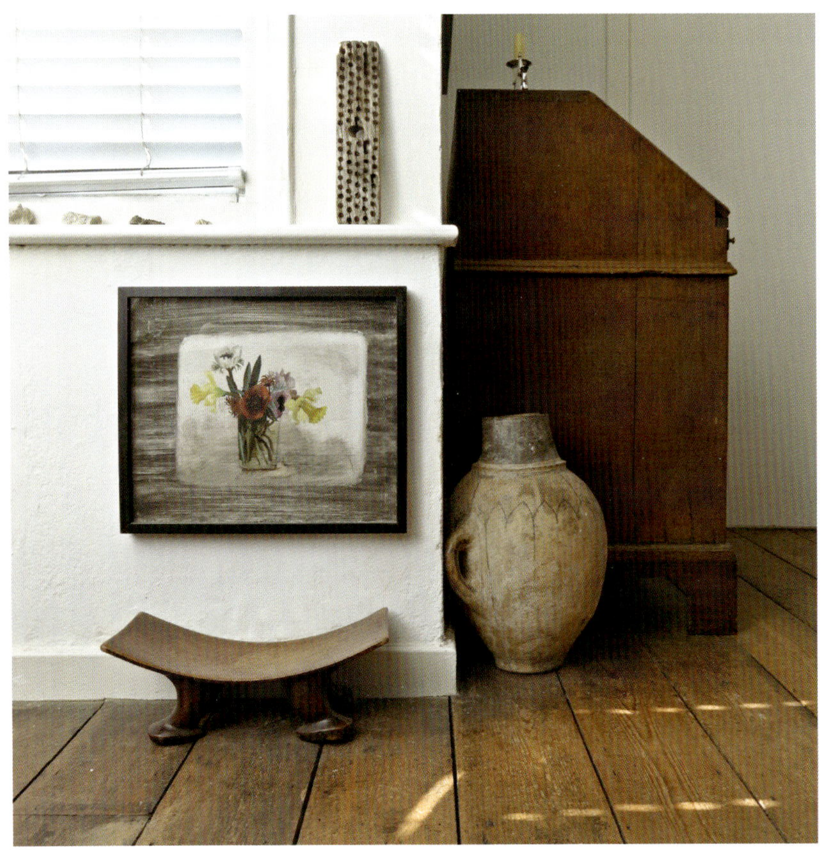

Flowers by Christopher Wood brings the right yellow and red into Kettle's Yard. The yellow is echoed across the room by a pale lemon on a seventeenth-century pewter dish. The jar is from Fez and the wooden pillow stool from an island off the coast of Africa. Jim Ede in *A Way of Life*

"His work is the crystallisation of a deep enjoyment of fundamental things and his ideas become alive – so living that when we see a place in one of his paintings you immediately wish to go there – you are there. Such vivacity of contact and such simple conveying of that contact through the medium of paint is I think the characteristic of a real painter … A great number of his paintings give me a renewed sense of the beauty of life and the reality of that beauty."

H.S. Ede, letter to *The Listener* regarding a review of Christopher Wood's work by Roger Hicks, published 16 March 1938

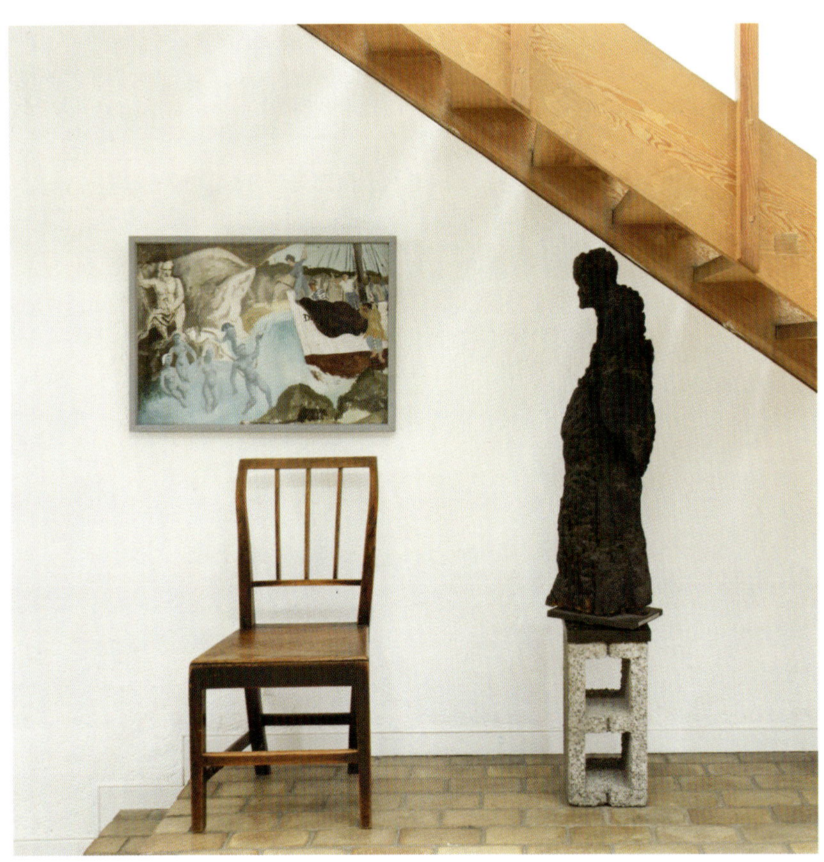

Ulysses and the Sirens (or Mermaids) in the house extension alongside a lightning-struck willow branch found by John Catto on the banks of the River Cam, he called it 'St Edmund'.

NOTES ON CHRISTOPHER WOOD

H.S. (Jim) Ede

Christopher Wood might reasonably be called the Constable of the Twentieth Century. Like all good artists he got a shock of joy out of the reality of what he saw, coming upon him with a vivid intensity, absorbing his whole nature, through that strange miracle which is art, directly symbolising the most significant realities of things represented, and as with Constable this is arrived at after constant study of nature itself. Art has come to be a miracle though it is something innate in human beings, stifled by the pressure of civilisation, of existing. Kit Wood, in his good moments, allowed no stifling of his sweeping joyous contact with visual reality and his work is supremely rational. He painted in order to put down, in his enthusiasm, the reality of the thing he saw, an expression springing directly from his need to say "I love this" and not from any motive of boasting a technical dexterity. It was natural to him to paint, taking to it, as to all he did, with a simple directness. To paint a picture, to eat a dinner, to talk with a friend, to do a thousand other things was but to LIVE … and he lived more dangerously than most.

"I love ships" he said, "they have such interesting lives". His vast interest in his subject makes us interested too. His paintings retain a sense of wonder, wonder which is at the root of all art. This excited and exciting vigour clamoured for expression making him impatient of detail in anxiety to grasp the intensity of the whole before it fled him or he it. He couldn't state his feelings in a fumbling inadequate manner, it was too exciting for that and carried all before it. A warmth of humanity nourishes his vision and he invites us to share this warmth. A bunch of flowers is a bunch of flowers, smell it; a street is a street, walk up it.

In a letter describing the country around Mount Etna he broke off with "What a country, too poetical to be described by an Englishman although we are the greatest poets in Europe and feel things in our own northern way more than Italians, but dare not say so". Christopher Wood dared more than most, he painted without hesitation or embarrassment, straight from the heart, and like Gainsborough and early Constables, his pictures have that special English quality which makes of a painting the spiritual realisation, profoundly significant, of homely things. His problem is to create a parallel to visual facts and not an imitation: his subjects only excite his fancy by their pictorial significance. He loved trees and boats and the sea, and at once saw them as paintings. He had the power of interpretation in a high degree and an extraordinary perception of relevant matter. With his simple relationship to his medium, the actual statement follows almost automatically the trained instinct. By his simplifications nothing is lost, everything is gained, and by his remarkable sense of tone he gives authority to his simplest statements.

There is a large self-portrait of 1927 at Kettle's Yard "painted from memory like a fairy prince" he told someone in a letter. He is surrounded by Paris from the windows of the studio, dressed in his harlequin jersey and Breton trousers, the familiar objects of his life by his side, paints, pipe and lighter. There is an emphasis on the hands and face which makes the human element the one which dominates the picture. It is himself, painting himself in the material world of his own studio.

A talking brush Kit Wood had and talk which is alive from corner to corner of his canvas, an easy manipulation of paint, free, but never showy or slick. He does not clutter his ideas with irrelevant furnishing. Indeed so truly is he master of the situation that he can leave large restful spaces for the eye to dwell upon – spaces held by the force of his intention.

In *Boat Building* we can see these spaces, but so clear is the bone structure of the picture, that we are unaware of them. The facts are so exactly stated that the whole story is before us at a glance. He was very impressed by the sadness of this scene, skeletons of the fishermen who would take them out to sea and not return. Mothers and wives, who had sent their sons – their husbands, helping a younger generation to build new ships of death. I see this in his thought since he wrote of it in a letter. How pictorially he has visualised it; without a shade of sentimentality. It is a clear straight statement, vigorous and human, which belongs to that very English world of such clear statements as Shakespeare's sonnets. This was painted two months before his death.

A little earlier he was writing "my brain, life, work, everything is a maelstrom at the moment. I can't explain it. I work at a terrific speed and force, but at the same time in a sort of trance, not knowing exactly what I am doing, and yet making every super-human effort of brain and body. Sometimes I work from ten

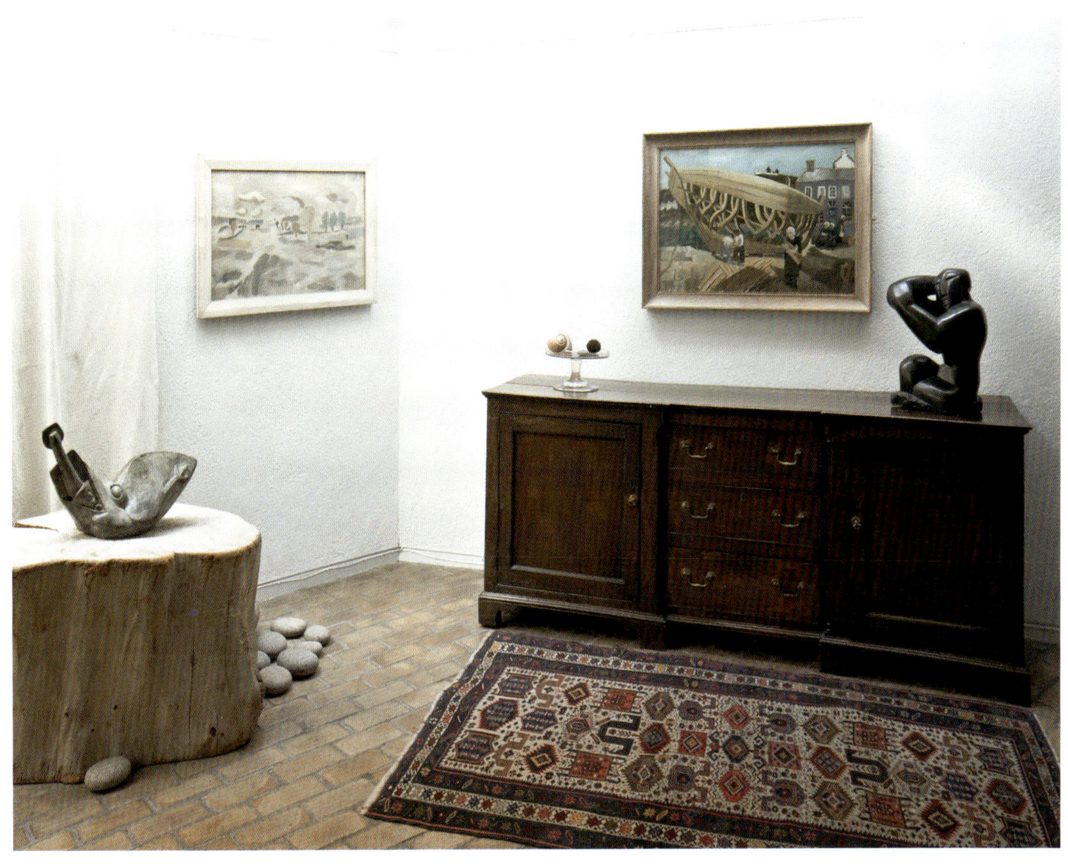

Wood's ***Building the Boat, Tréboul*** in the house extension. Also seen Henri Gaudier-Brzeska's ***Bird Swallowing a Fish*** (1914) and ***Seated Woman*** (1914) with Ben Nicholson's ***Snowscape*** (c.1927).

in the morning to five in the evening, literally without stopping to look at what I am doing, as I am so terribly absorbed. This complete lack of sense of what is going on around me, after which I stop my work I am frightened by the smallest event that breaks in on my complete privacy of reflection".

There is a painting called *La Phare* [sic] which seems to me to show his appreciation of Alfred Wallis, yet in no way diminishes the full flavour of his own personality. It represents a dark sea with two little boats, and on the sands a white newspaper with whiter playing cards. There is a strong and clear stating of the abstract, a quality which comes first in the making of a work of art. It is essentially a thing of itself; it is the sea in terms of paint; it is the world of the artist's thought conveyed through the close juxtaposing of his light and shade – these exquisite whites on white, darks on dark, revolving in their own mystery as simply as the world itself revolves.

Christopher Wood's work shows a deep respect for something outside himself, – the world, the universe, good, sorrow, joy; he recognises instinctively and clearly some objective reality, and his own relation to it. He is responsive to the sensuous, the whole outside world in which he lives; responsive with a certain plainness, and direct normal sanity. He accepts much, and has a rich humour and humility, but his choices are determined by his organisation as an artist, and not by any code of morality or philosophy. He had a zest for life, and an untroubled implicit faith in it; a faith and aliveness which would persist even if he visited Hell, instinctively relying on some rightness at the heart of the universe which will unfailingly guide, direct and support. He was, I think, perpetually surprised, and ready always for new ways. To Winifred Nicholson he wrote: "But an ugly thing, at first sight, often turns out radiantly beautiful, if one gives it a little consideration and a good look."

Seamen and Mermaids [*Ulysses and the Sirens*] perhaps his last work and perhaps unfinished, is an unusual one for Wood, for it is painted out of his imagination and is not a parallel to visual facts. Perhaps it is symbolic of his temporal end, this phantom ship which may be the ship he had so loved all his life and has so often painted. These phantom sailors, alive, still, for him as they man the yards and glide, from his living world; the outside world of air and sunlight; into the unseen, eternal place which is to us limited to here and now.

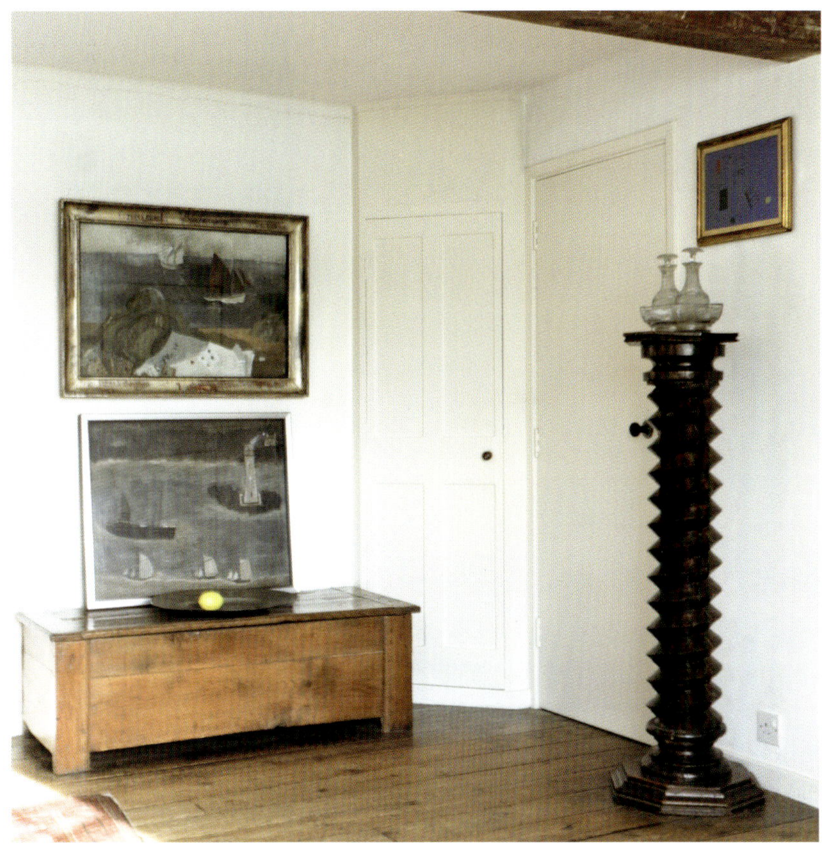

Wallis' ***Seascape*** (c.1928) sits beneath Christopher Wood's painting ***Le Phare*** in the dining room. ***Seascape*** was bought by Christopher Wood, who became a passionate advocate of Wallis. The two works are displayed together as Wood had them at his home in Minton Place, London.

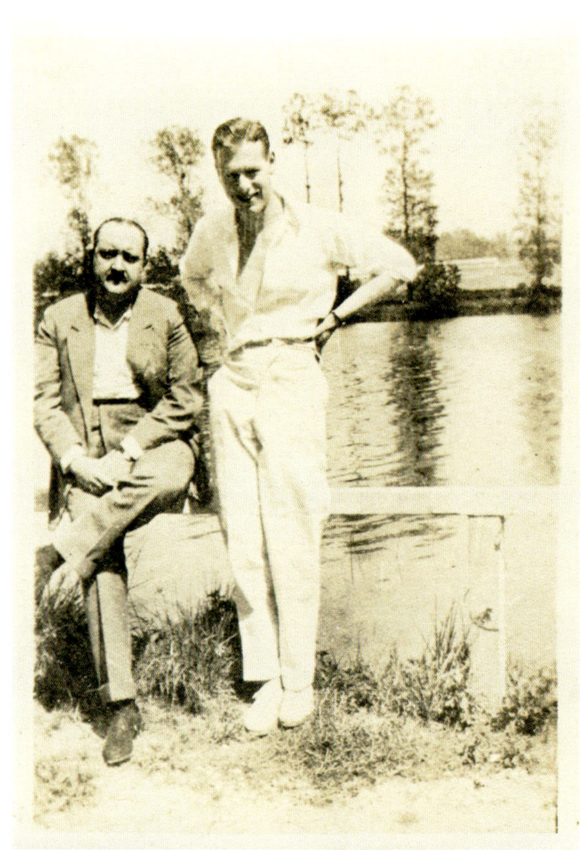

Alphonse Kahn (left) with Christopher Wood

CHRISTOPHER WOOD: PORTRAIT OF AN ARTIST

Elizabeth Fisher and Jane Morgans

THE STORY OF WOOD'S LIFE is one of self-creation. John Christopher Wood ('Kit' as he was more commonly known) was born in 1901, in Liverpool. He was the son of a doctor and grew up during the First World War, although he saw little of the suffering of those young men just a few years older than him, who went off to fight but did not return from the war. At 14, he contracted septicaemia, an illness that confined him to bed for three years and subsequently left him with a limp for the rest of his life. It was during this time that Kit and his mother developed a special bond, which continued throughout his life. He also took up drawing. In 1918, he went to study medicine at Malvern College, probably to please his father; after one term he enrolled at Liverpool University to study architecture but abandoned his education to move to London before the end of his first year. He was 19, and took a job working for an importer of dried fruit.

His route to and from work took him through the West End, passed the legendary cafés and bars still steeped in the bohemian atmosphere of the pre-war years. Here, Wood could sit sketching for hours, and observe the comings and goings of London life. Local clientele included artistic celebrities such as Wyndham Lewis and Augustus John, who became a friend and supporter of Wood. Wood's new acquaintances encouraged him to look across the Channel for inspiration. One of these was the art collector Alphonse Kahn, one of the best-connected men in the Paris art world, who invited him to visit him in Paris in 1921. Wood wrote to his mother to tell her of his plans:

> "Dearest Mother, you ask me what I am going to do: I have decided to try and be the greatest painter that has ever lived."
>
> Letter from Christopher Wood to Clare Wood, October 1921

In the 1920s, Paris was an extraordinary place to be, exhilarating for the affluent and artistically inclined. Anxious to shrug off the austerity and trauma of the First World War, the city became renowned for its hedonistic and liberal attitudes, and artists and writers from all over the world gravitated to the city. The roaring Twenties, or Années folles, were the high-water mark of Surrealism, Dada and other modern art movements, and Paris was at the centre of the European avant-garde.

Wood's boyish good looks and public-school Englishness certainly eased his entrance into the fashionable social and artistic circles of Paris. Winifred Nicholson paints a highly romanticised picture: "He walked with the speed and spring and vitality of boyhood, of more than that, of someone who has been a part of the great wild nature for a whole long day, and read her silly gay secrets with the power of eternal youth." (Letter to Frosca Munster, 1930) Wood was a charismatic, wide-eyed Englishman abroad, full of life and apparent innocence. His limp, when it was noticed, only added to his appeal; it made him poignantly vulnerable. Jean Cocteau wrote about it in his poem, *Kit*:

"This limp of his is puzzling in an angel,
The weight of only one foot on the earth"

Initially, Wood stayed with Kahn in his Bois de Boulogne apartment in the 16th arrondissement, and enrolled at the Académie Julian. Through Kahn, Wood was introduced to a sophisticated circle that included Eugenia Errazuriz, a wealthy socialite who had supported Picasso in his early days, and her nephew, the Chilean diplomat Antonio de Gandarillas. Gandarillas was a notorious figure: a South American émigré living in Paris, who was married but saw little of his family, preferring the more risqué set of younger men. Before long, Gandarillas adopted Wood as his protégé and lover. They moved in together in 1922. Their relationship provided crucial financial support for Wood, and Gandarillas' wealth and connections, heady social lifestyle and passion for gambling, travel and art ensured that Wood, as his companion, enjoyed the refinements, privileges and excesses of the beau monde.

Wood's early connections proved fruitful for his development as a painter too. Through Gandarillas and his aunt, Wood met Picasso in 1923. Wood regarded

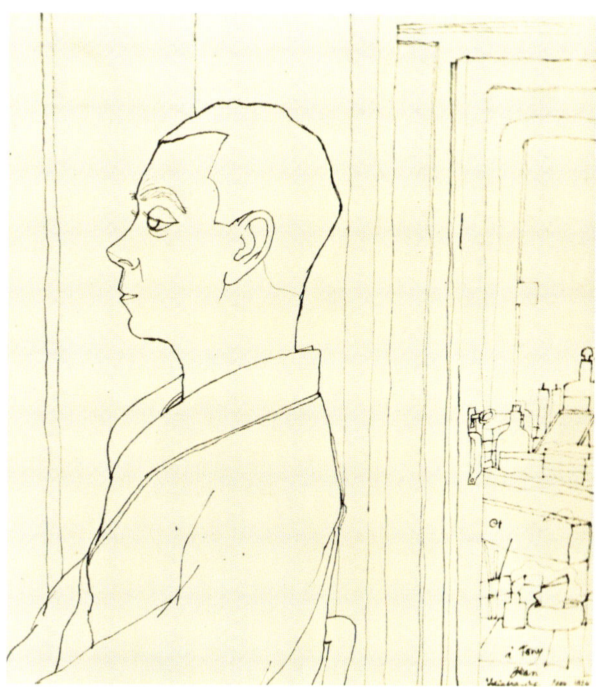

Drawing of Tony Gandarillas by Jean Cocteau, 1926

Picasso as "the greatest painter of the day" and was eager to learn from him. Picasso was unusually generous with the young English artist: he gave Wood advice on his work, and from Picasso Wood learnt an understanding of line, colour relationships and even the use of housepaint. Wood particularly admired the older artist's ability to assimilate influences from a variety of sources. It was not until 1926 that Picasso visited his studio. Wood reported it to his mother:

> "It was a terrible moment for me as it is what I have dreaded for a long time, but it had to happen before I could make any headway here … I feel as if a terrible weight has been lifted off my shoulder. Curiously enough it has given me enormous self confidence, the fact of his having seen them, and I feel much better disposed towards the future."
>
> Letter from Christopher Wood to Clare Wood, 2 February 1926

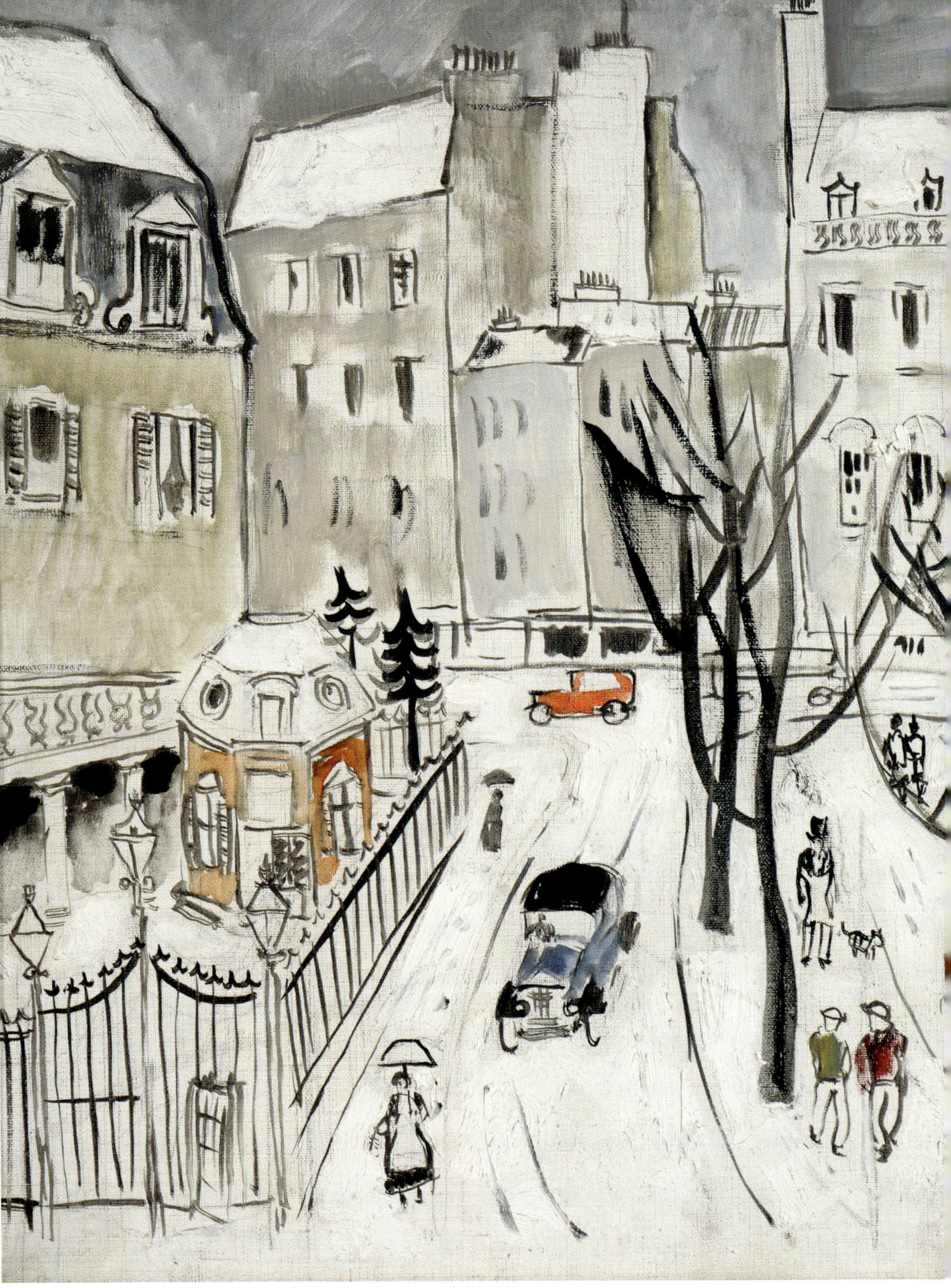

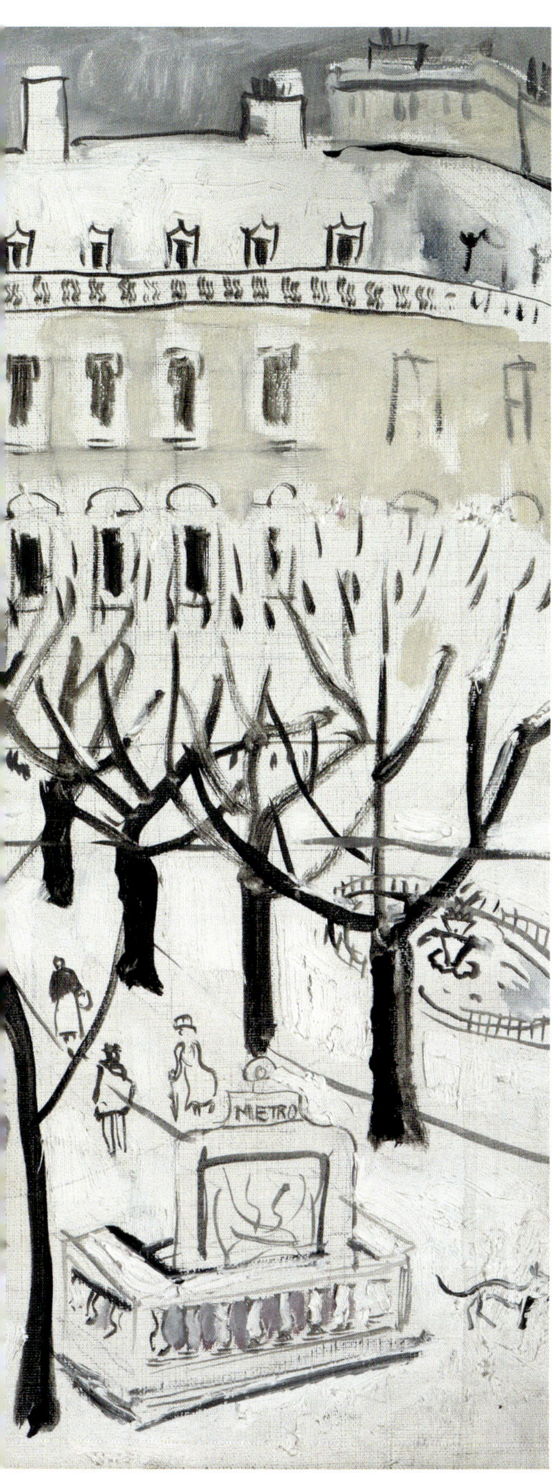

Paris Snow Scene, 1926
Oil on canvas, 450 x 545 mm

Gandarillas' passion for travelling took them both away from Paris frequently and for long periods. Their trips often developed along the way, financed by Gandarillas' success at the casinos. They travelled around the Mediterranean, to North Africa, Greece, Turkey, Italy, and across Europe, through Germany, Austria, Spain and the south of France. During the summer months, Wood and Gandarillas were regular passengers on 'Le Train Bleu', a luxury overnight express train from Paris to the French Riviera. Emblematic of fashionable Paris society, 'Le Train Bleu' inspired a popular ballet produced by the ballet impresario Sergei Diaghilev in 1924. It drew together an impressive roll-call of artistic heavyweights: the libretto was by Jean Cocteau, music by Darius Milhaud, set designs were by Henri Laurens, curtains by Pablo Picasso, and costumes designed by Coco Chanel.

Diaghilev's company the Ballets Russes, and the regular flight of the beau monde to the Côte d'Azur on 'Le Train Bleu' epitomised the decadence of the Twenties. In chic resorts along the Riviera from Marseille to Monte Carlo, Wood and Gandarillas coincided with other major figures from the Paris avant-garde: when they were in Villefranche, Jean Cocteau was also in town – as were Francis Poulenc, Georges Auric, Stravinsky, Ernest Hemingway, F. Scott Fitzgerald and Diaghilev, Isadora Duncan, Max Jacob and René Crevel. In Marseille, they stayed in the same hotel as Picasso and the principal dancers of the Ballets Russes.

Early in 1926, Wood and Gandarillas were in Monte Carlo, where Diaghilev was also staying. Diaghilev began to toy with the idea of commissioning Wood as a designer for the Ballets Russes production of *Romeo and Juliet*. The ballet was to be set as a rehearsal, a behind-the-scenes view of the Shakespearian play, and not the theatrical work itself. This was a great coup for the young British artist. He joined a prestigious line of designers that included Matisse, Picasso, Rouault, Utrillo and Derain. However, the artist's working relationship with Diaghilev was stormy and, taking the advice of both Cocteau and Picasso, Wood refused to change his designs according to Diaghilev's wishes. In the argument that ensued, Wood resigned and Diaghilev commissioned Max Ernst and Joan Miró to design the scenery, a move that provoked a riot from the Surrealists on the opening night in Paris – in protest at the involvement of two of their number with the 'gangster capitalist' Diaghilev.

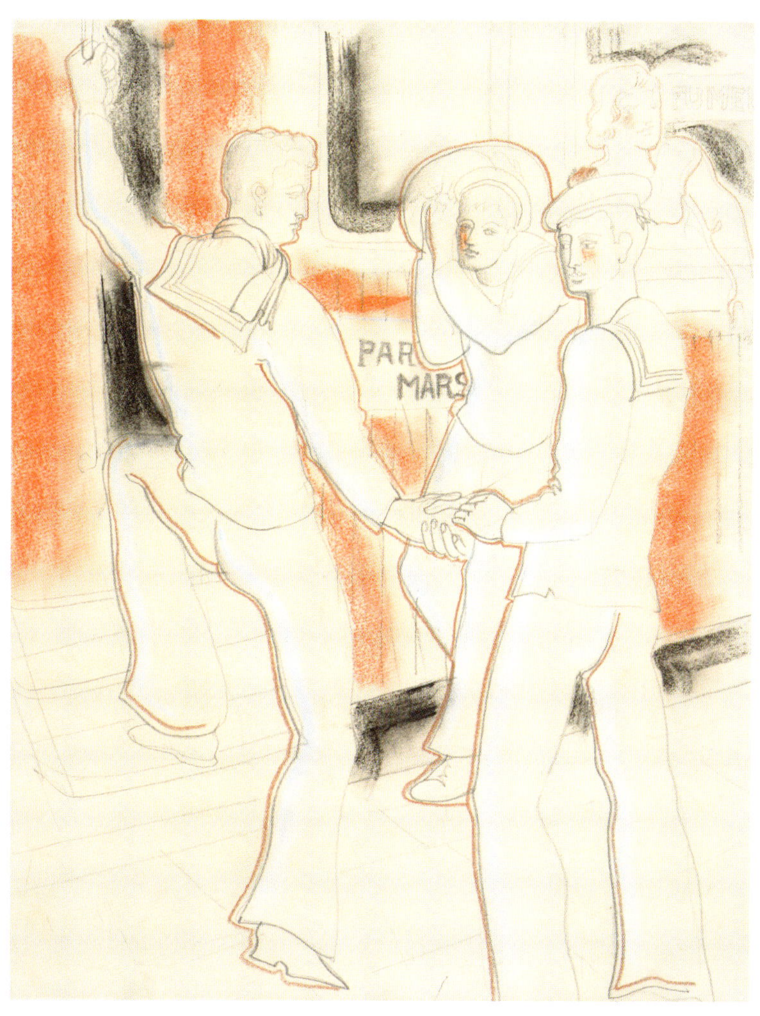

Les Trois Marins, undated. Pencil and pastel on paper, 334 x 260 mm
Courtesy of the University of Essex

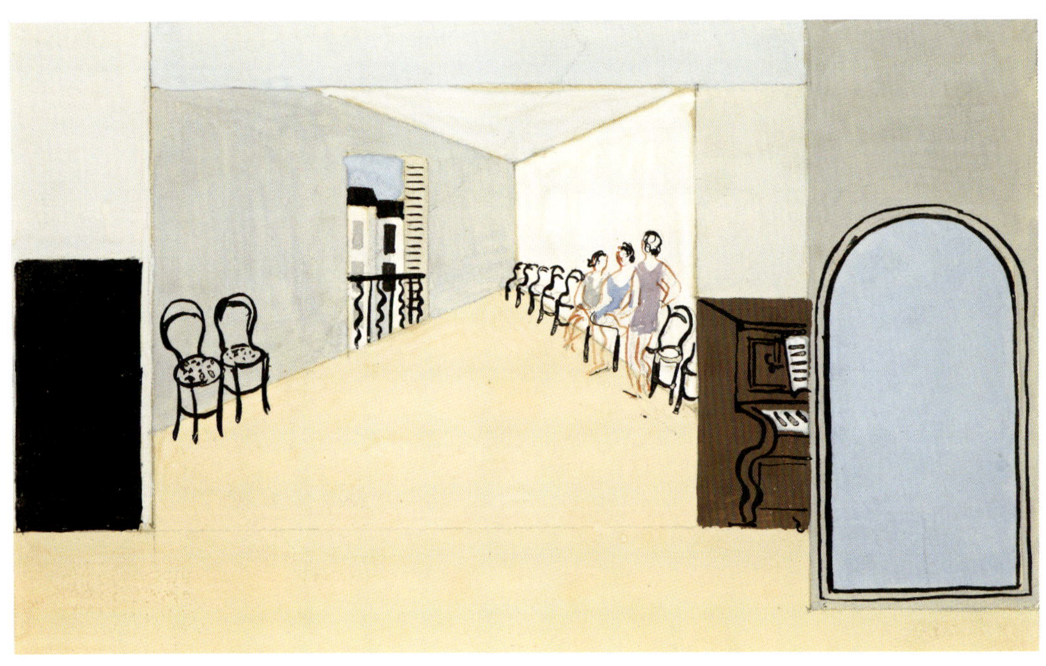

Stage designs for Diaghilev's ballet ***Romeo and Juliet*** (scene one), 1925
Gouache on paper, each 140 x 235 mm

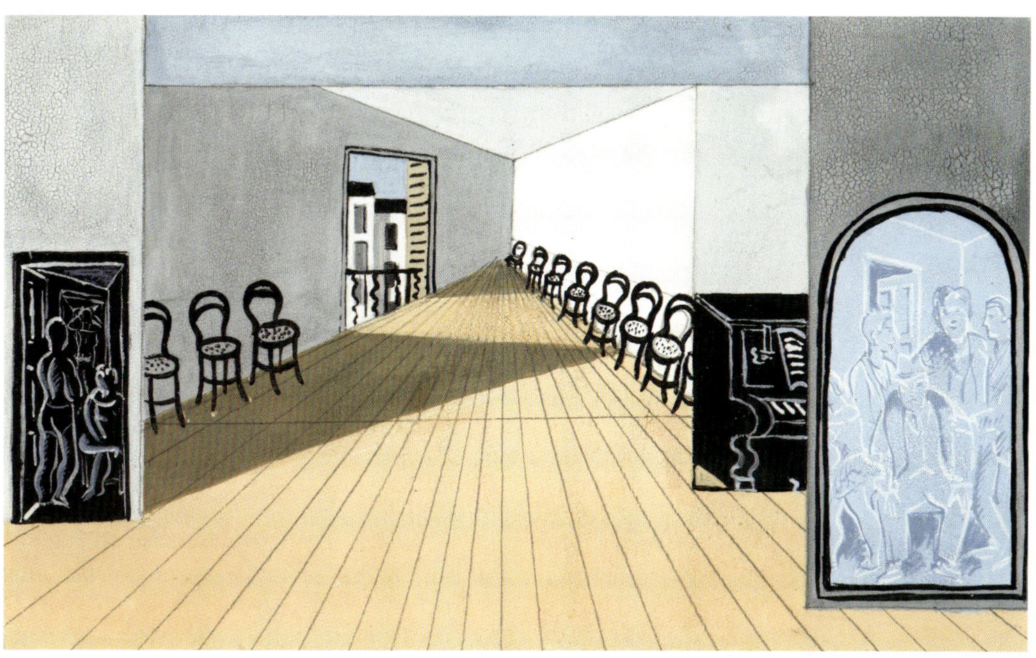

"Picasso is charming to me and said he could not understand why Diaghilev had not taken my ballet, that it simply could not have been better or more beautiful. He loves it and simply could not make out why it had been refused."

Letter from Christopher Wood to Clare Wood, 2 February 1926

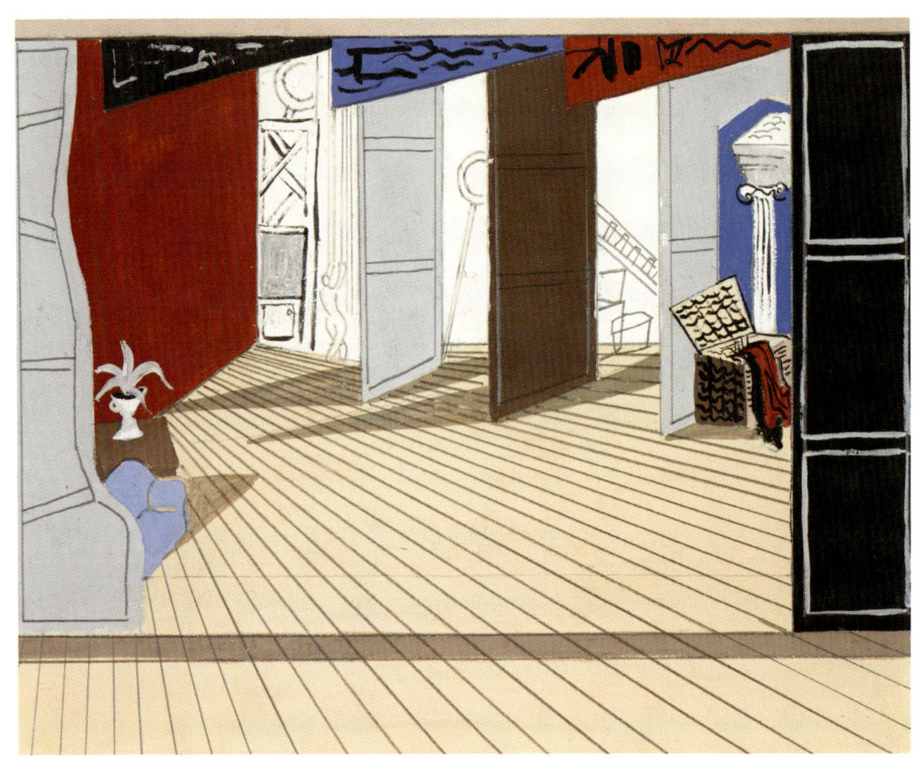

Stage designs for Diaghilev's ballet ***Romeo and Juliet*** (scene two), 1925
Gouache on paper, 200 x 250 mm and 290 x 410 mm

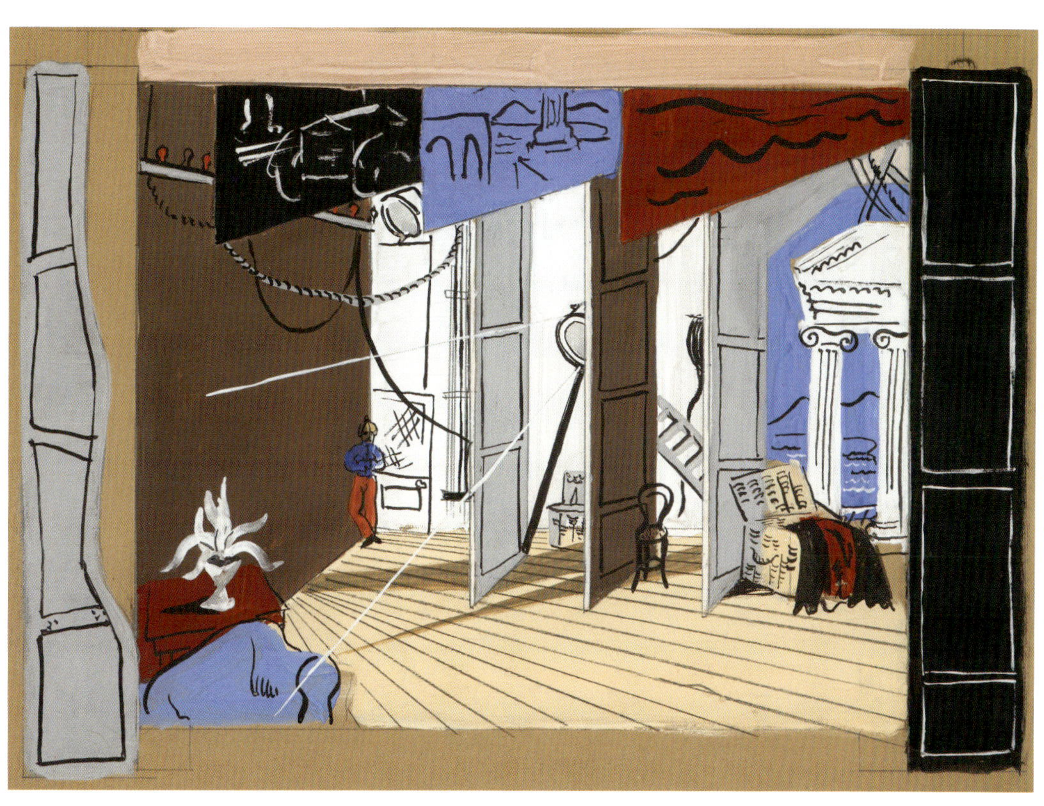

WOOD MET JEAN COCTEAU at the Hôtel Welcome in Villefranche on the Riviera in 1924. Cocteau's lover, a young writer named Raymond Radiguet, had recently died of Typhoid fever at the age of 20. Wood was immediately in awe of Cocteau, and enjoyed a brief period as the poet's new 'pet' protégé. Wood invited Cocteau to share his studio in Paris later that year, an arrangement which suited both, as Wood was an early worker and Cocteau preferred the evening. Cocteau encouraged and supported Wood and, through Cocteau's teaching, learnt the trick of making drawings with a single line. Under Cocteau's influence, Wood also became a regular user of opium.

Jean Bourgoint was one of several handsome young men who inhabited Jean Cocteau's circle. Cocteau later based the main characters in his novel *Les Enfants Terribles* on Jean and his sister Jeanne. They were unusually close for siblings, and lived together, sharing a bedroom in their mother's flat. Jean succeeded Wood in Cocteau's affections and was also a lover of both Jean Hugo and Jacques Maritain. Jeanne was a model for the fashion designer Edward Molyneux, and dressed as a 'garçonne', or woman dressed as a man, which was the height of fashion at the time. The styles were deliberately shapeless and tomboyish.

The Bourgoint's ambiguous sexuality appealed to Wood, and he was particularly attracted by Jeanne's distinctively tomboyish looks. A brief but intense affair between Jeanne and Wood began in 1926. In August, Wood travelled with Gandarillas to Cornwall, where he stayed for 6 weeks. From there he wrote to Jeanne:

> "my adorable little hare … my dear little darling … my dearest little friend … my little sweetheart … my dear little Jeanne … I love you terribly, I know because I have become so firm in my mind about you. I do not hesitate to tell you that you are the only woman for me …."
>
> Letter from Christopher Wood to Jeanne Bourgoint, undated

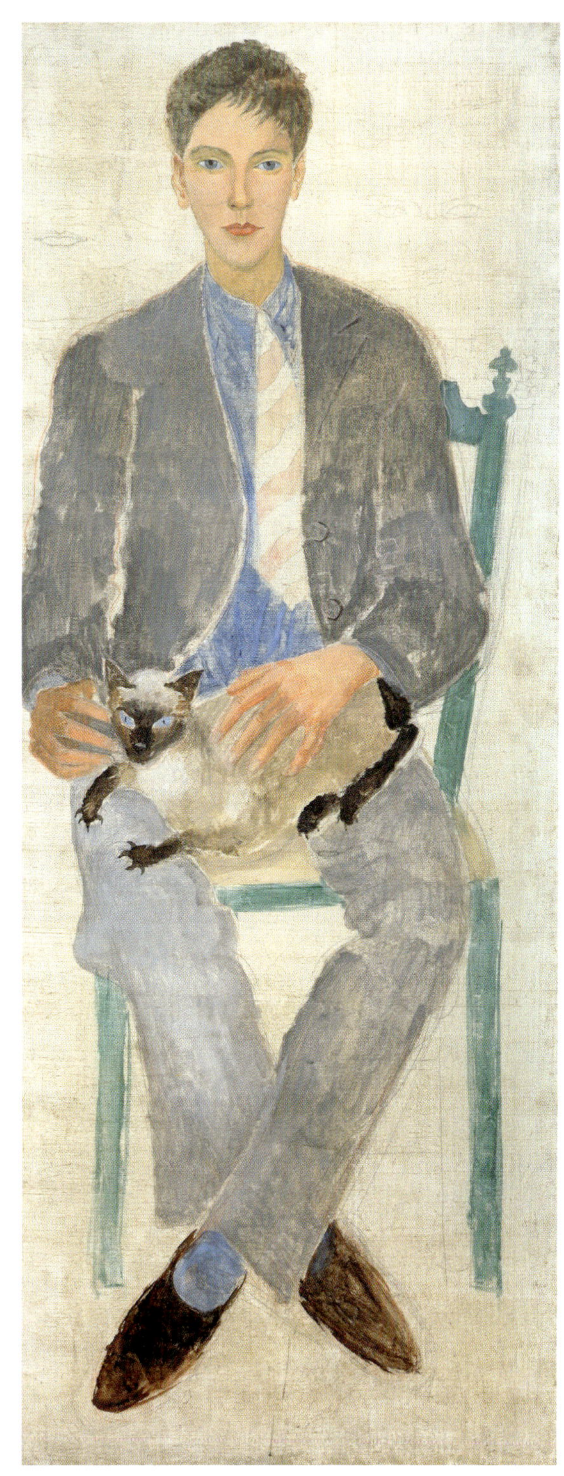

Boy with Cat (Jean Bourgoint), 1926
Oil and graphite on canvas,
1480 x 585 mm (detail overleaf)
Bequest of Libby Holman Reynolds, 1974

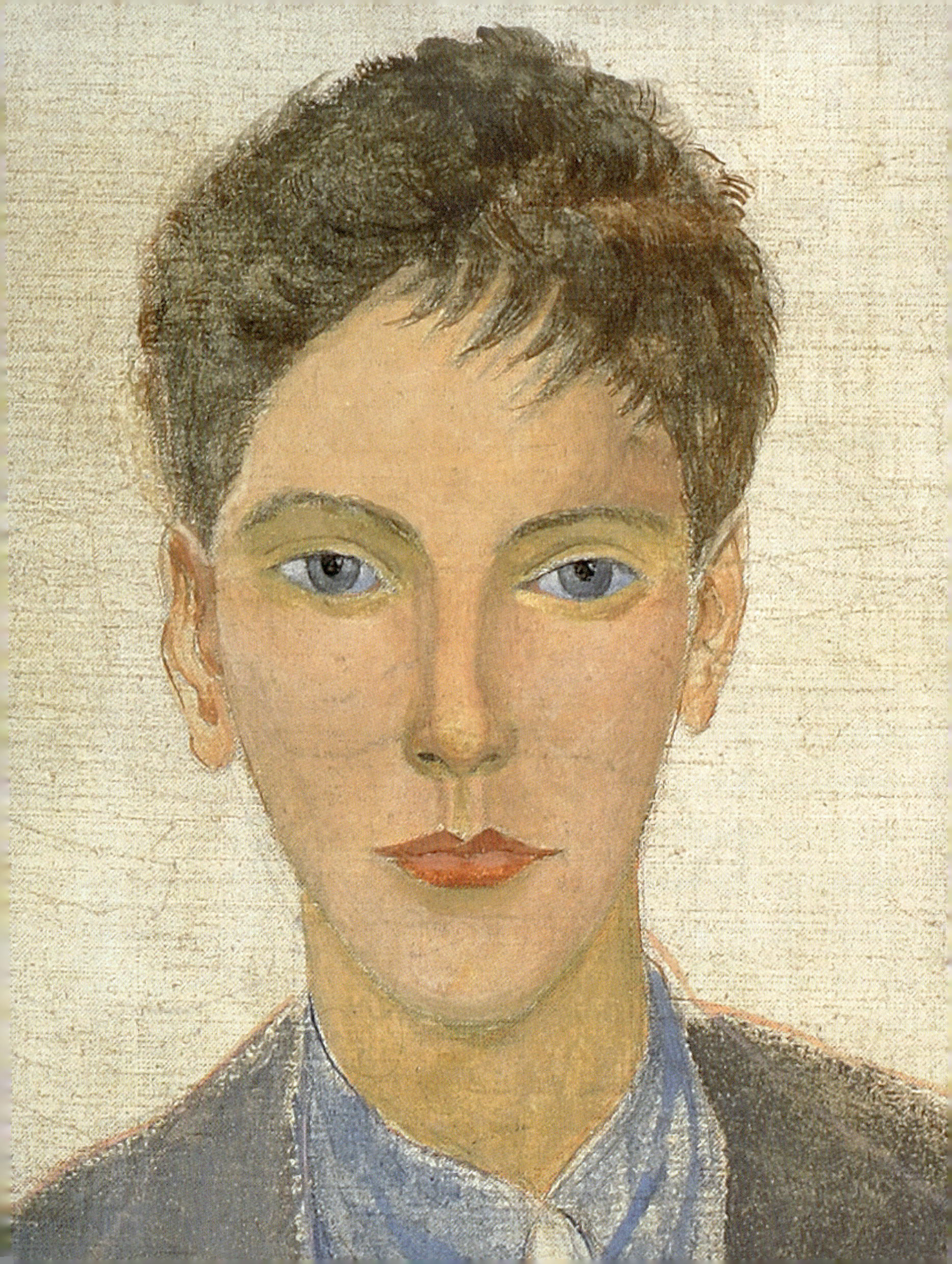

Wood's portraits of the Bourgoints invoke the simmering sexuality of the fey youths of Cocteau's circle. In the tradition of Leonardo da Vinci's *Lady with an Ermine* (1489-90) and Hans Holbein The Younger's *Lady with a Squirrel* (1526-8), the artist depicts the sitters with an animal companion, symbolic of their character. The Siamese cat, whose blue eyes match exactly the blue of Jean's own eyes, suggests a thinly veiled feline sexuality (traditionally cats have symbolised fickleness and promiscuity) while the red fox pelt on Jeanne's lap was a sign of high taste and luxury in fashion. Traditionally associated with cunning trickery, or possessing magical powers, the fox also lent a wild edge to Jeanne's demure pose.

“The door opened wide to reveal a girl of sixteen, with a strong physical resemblance to Paul. She had the same blue eyes shadowed by dark lashes, the same pallor of complexion. But whereas the lines of his face betrayed a certain weakness of comparison, hers, two years older, beneath soft curling hair, had already ceased to be a sketch for the finished portrait, was already groping for its organic principle and racing, dishevelled, to overtake its beauty.”

Cocteau, Jean, *Les Enfant Terribles*,
translated by Rosamond Lehmann, London: Vintage, 2011, p.17

Mlle Bourgoint, 1929. Oil on canvas, 995 x 635 mm
Courtesy of the University of Essex

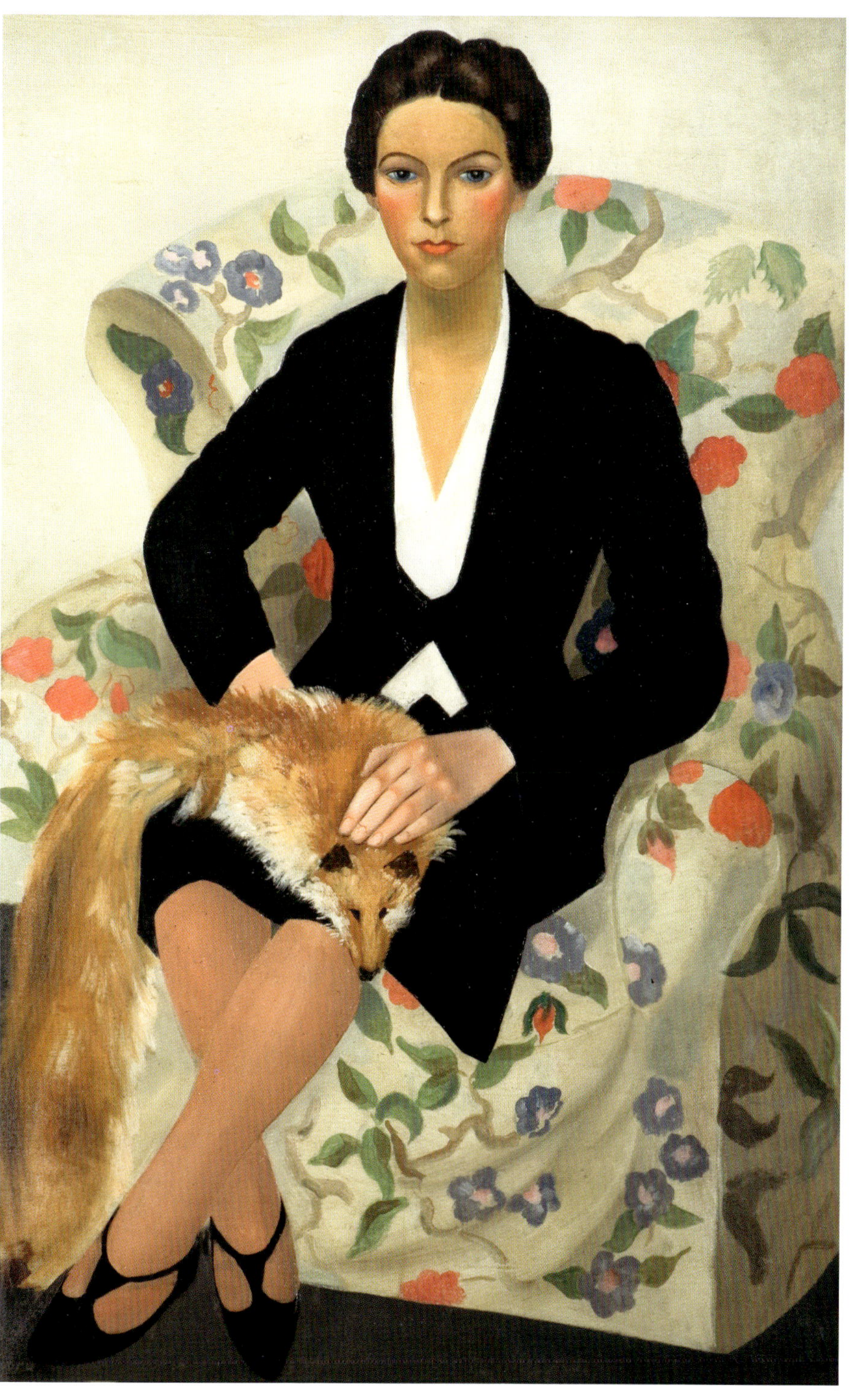

IN THE SPRING OF 1927, Wood wrote to Winifred Nicholson "I have never worked so hard before, and am really having a life and death struggle with it never as I knew before .... So many ideas crush my brain that I seem never able to contemplate one than a thousand others disturb it." (Letter to Winifred Nicholson, undated). In April, Wood took part in an exhibition alongside Ben and Winifred Nicholson and William Staite-Murray at Beaux Arts in London. The show passed without making much of a splash although it included one significant work, recently finished – a large self-portrait. In the introduction to the catalogue of the Beaux-Arts exhibition, Jean Cocteau wrote:

> "If I was not Wood's friend, I would want to be having seen his paintings .... In Christopher Wood there is no malice. There is frankness, a naivety – the goodness of a young dog that has not yet had the illness of the time .... If Christopher Wood wished to paint sleep he would not paint his dreams, but a man asleep, and this is an important difference, a return to the humanity to which the best of our youth is turning consciously or unconsciously. Wood is an English painter. His painting speaks little, it takes exercise in the fresh air, it has red cheeks and the huge hands of a sportsman. Before the canvases you don't think you live. No subtle problem poses itself here ... This unaccustomed frankness gives us a taste for life and a desire to really know this young painter whose eyes, since they reflect nothing false, give the lie to that Harlequin jumper."

Self Portrait, 1927. Oil on canvas, 1295 x 960 mm (detail overleaf)
Inscribed "lent to Clare Wood / Property of Jim Ede"

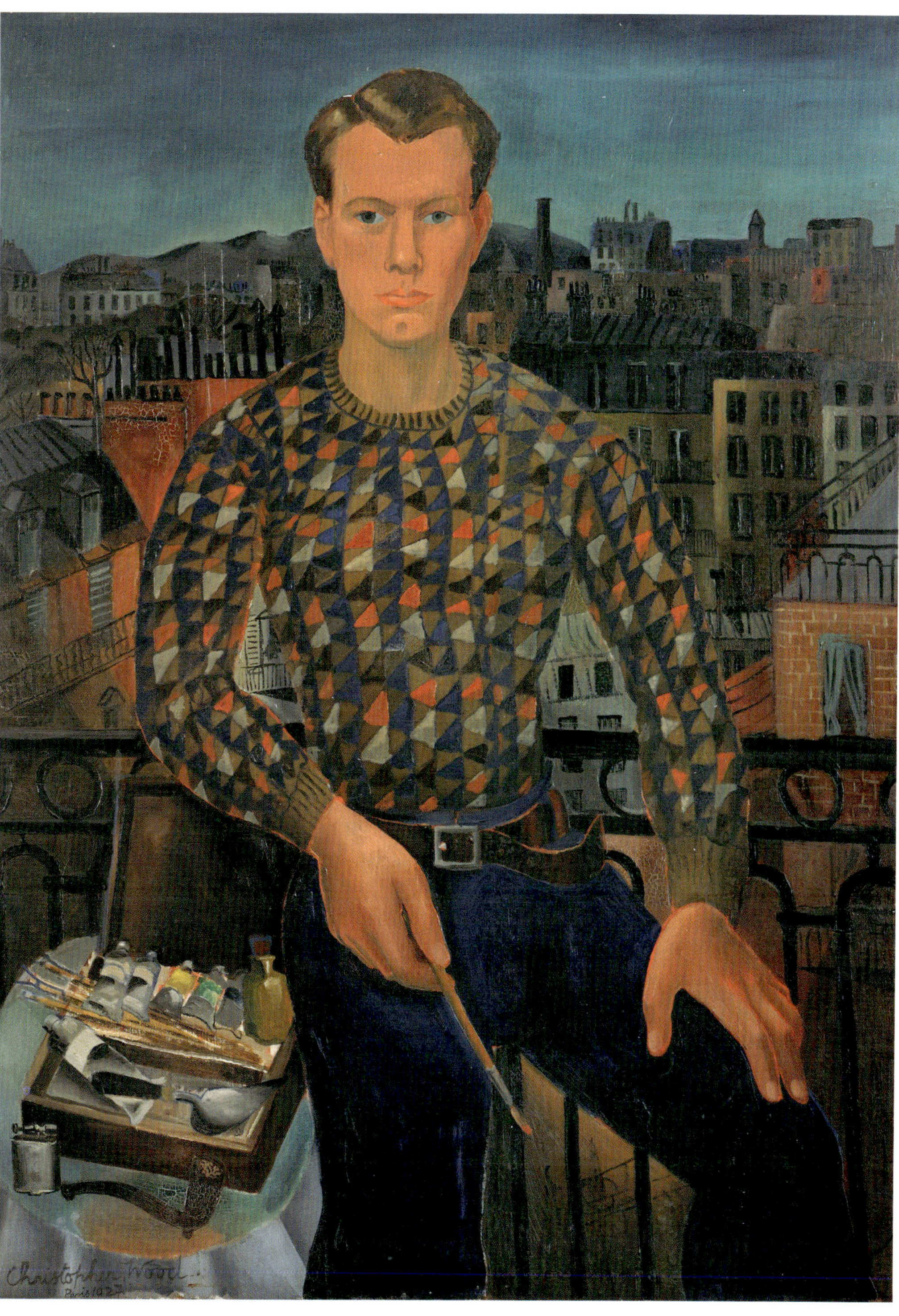
Christopher Wood.
Paris 1927

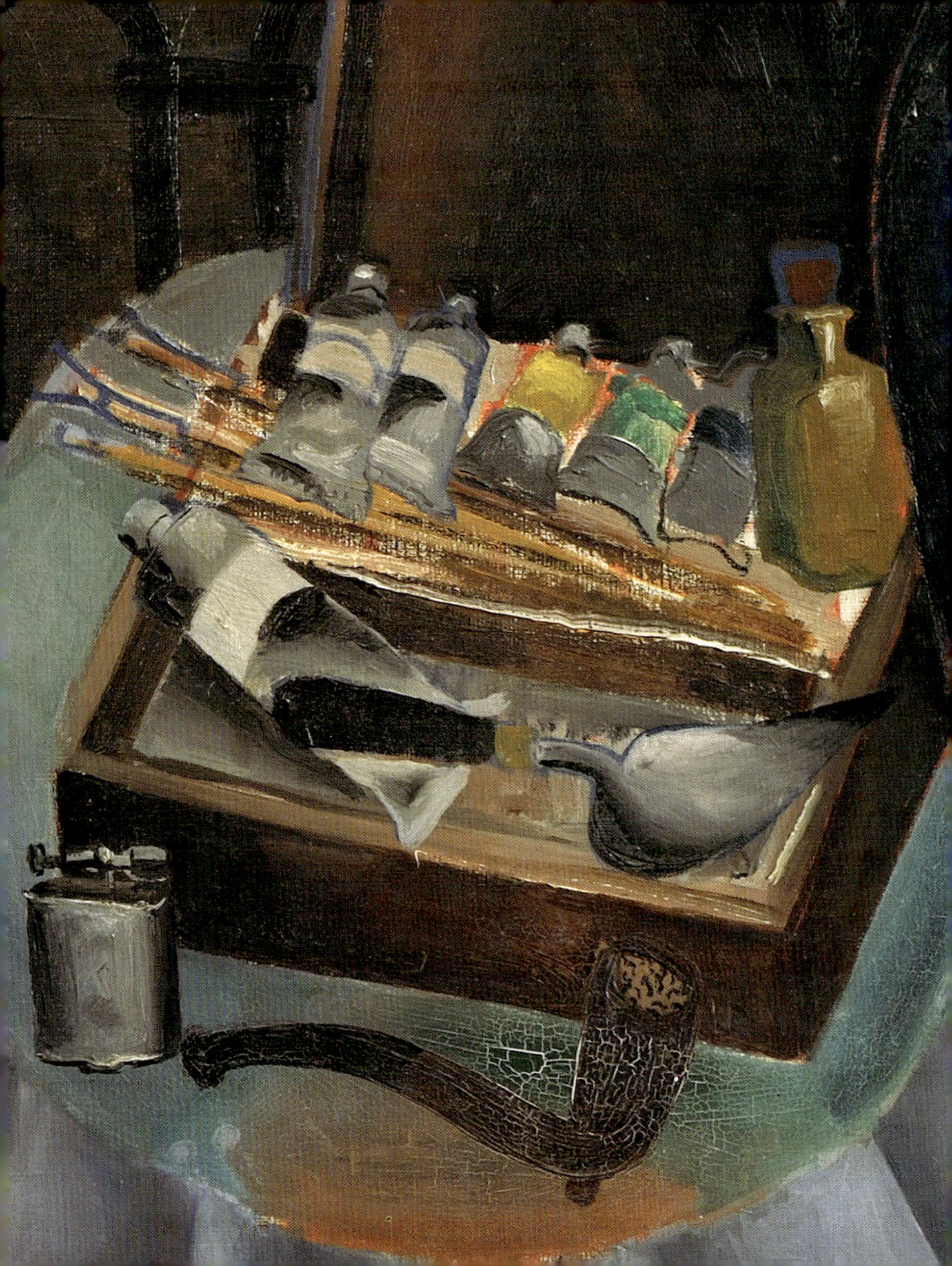

The roof-tops of Paris are the setting Wood chose for his second self portrait, looking out over the city that he loved and had been living in for six years. He surrounded himself with familiar objects: his opium pipe, lighter and paint box. He also chose to present himself wearing a densely patterned jumper, unmistakably evocative of the traditional motif of the harlequin. An iconic symbol in French culture, it was a motif that carried with it an association with French painting dating back over two hundred years. Picasso had used the harlequin in many works, particularly self-portraits, as too had Cezanne and others. In his first self-portrait, *Harlequin* (1925), Wood depicted himself in full harlequin costume. Wood self-consciously identified with the figure of the romantic, tragi-comic clown, but for an English painter to use this very French device, it was also a calculated move to align himself with his fellow artists in the Parisian avant-garde.

This painting also reveals Wood tackling some of the ideas about composition and colour relationships that he had encountered in Paris. Inspired by the works of Van Gogh and Picasso but also others including Gauguin, Seurat, Utrillo, Modigliani, Braque, he experimented with a variety of painting styles and techniques, rapidly learning the language of his French contemporaries. Here, Wood uses cubist techniques to explore the relationship between fore- and background, and the problem of depicting three dimensions on a two dimensional canvas. The resulting work shows Wood articulating a key modernist idea: that of the insistent physicality of the picture plane.

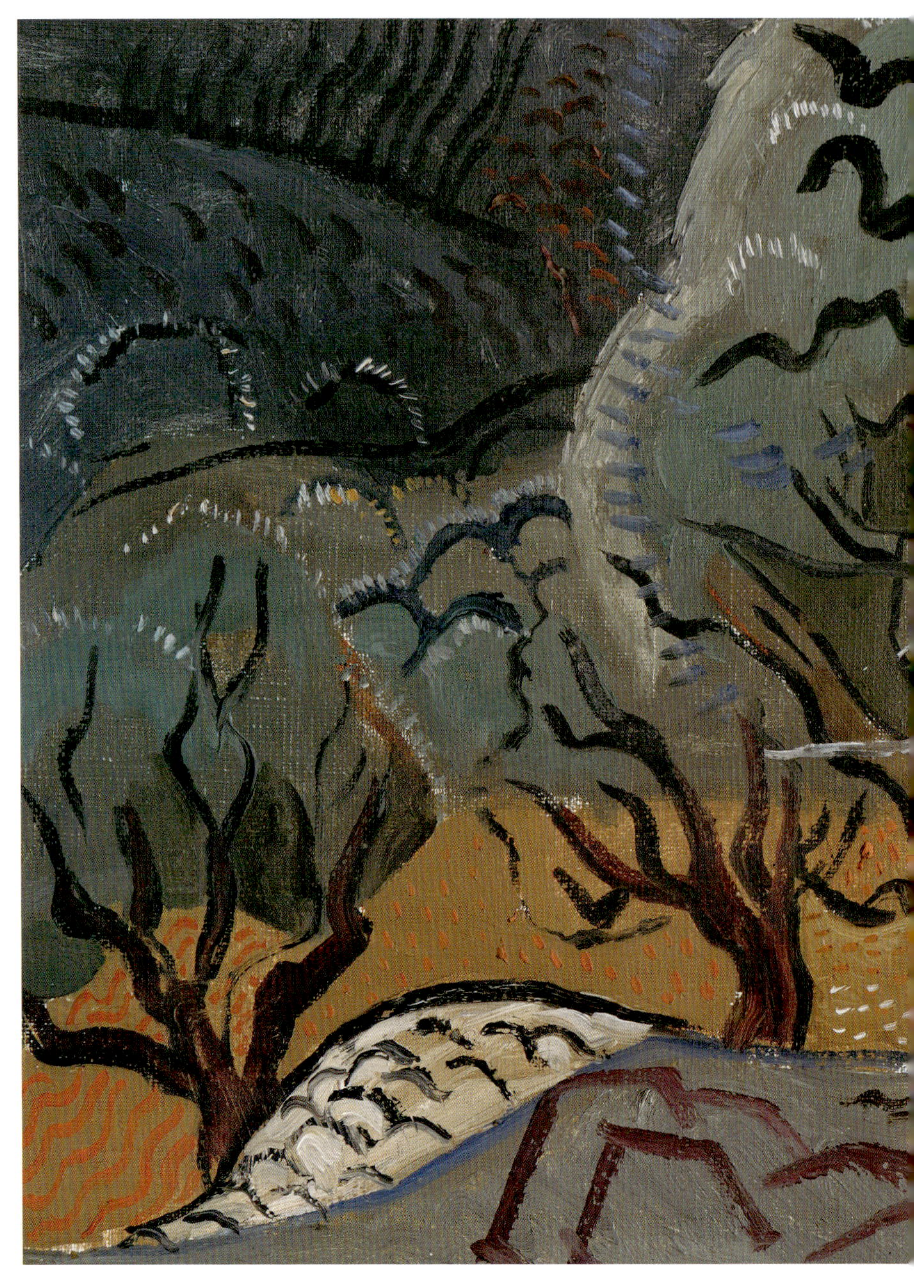

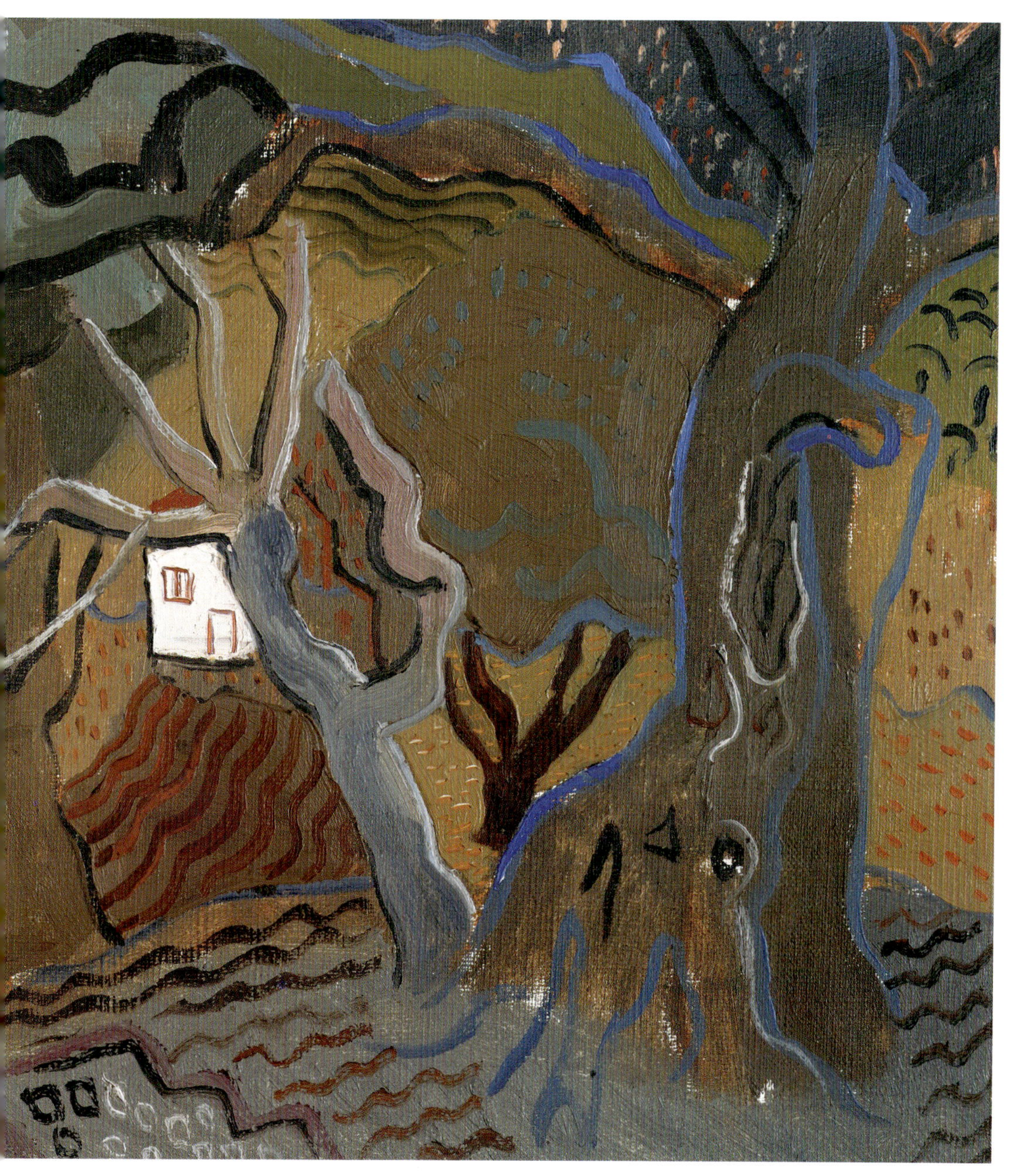

Landscape at Vence, Little White House, 1927. Oil on canvas, 260 x 450 mm
Gift from Christopher Wood. Inscribed "for my friend Jim Eade [sic] Christopher Wood 1928"

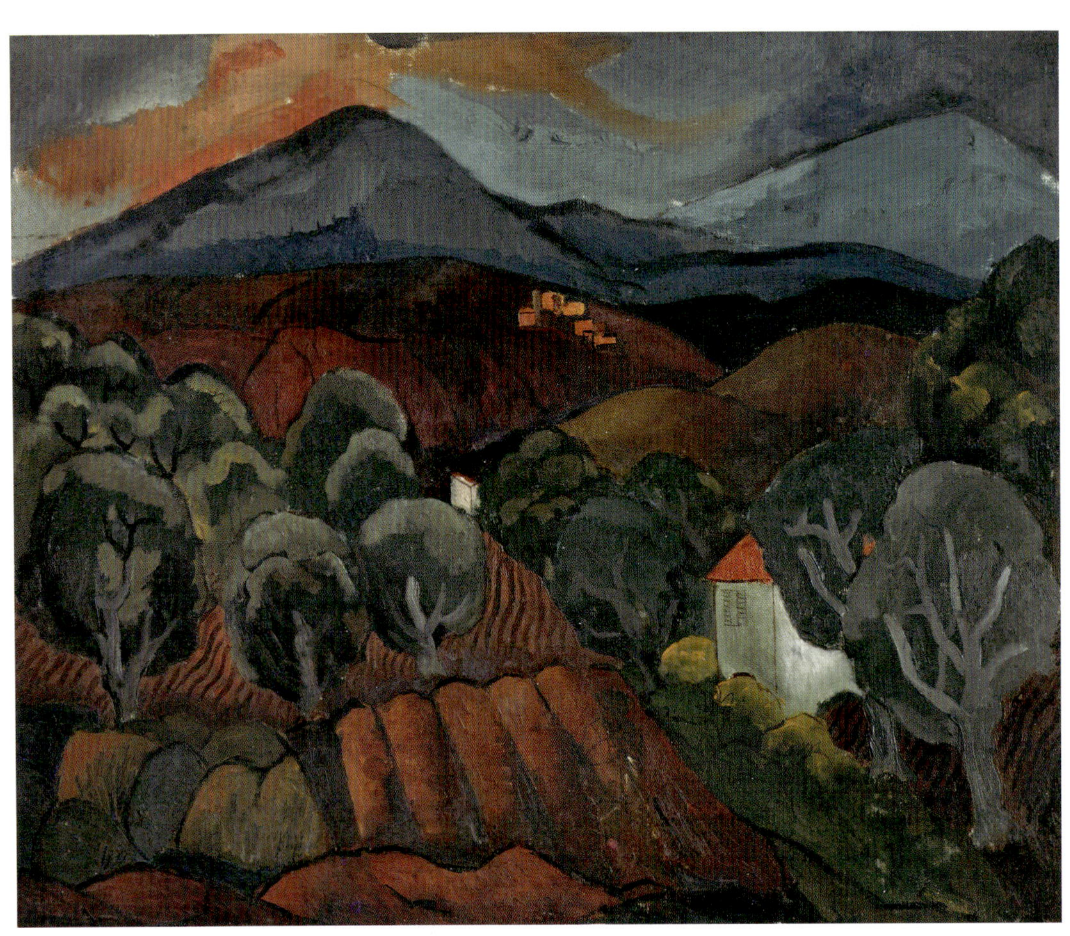

Landscape at Vence, 1927. Oil on canvas, 530 x 650 mm

Wood spent the rest of 1927 in the Mediterranean. In Cannes, he embarked on another affair, this time with Meraud Guinness, a painter who had studied at the Slade, then with Archipenko and Picabia in Paris. She was also the daughter of a wealthy American family, who did not approve of their daughter's romance with Wood. Meraud's mother intervened and they separated; in turmoil Wood sought out his old friend Gandarillas, who was in Marseille, nursing the writer René Crevel through tuberculosis. In intervals from nursing, Wood painted, and as Crevel's condition improved, they took him to the village of Vence in the hills behind Nice, in the south of France. It was at Vence that Wood's mood of post-Meraud gloom translated into dark colours and shades of black; from this palette he developed a distinctive feeling for psychological depth which became a characteristic of his mature style.

> "My pictures are getting darker and darker and so black. No black is black enough. I do wish I could finish my pictures as I begin them instead of spoiling them as I nearly always do now."
>
> Letter from Christopher Wood to Ben and Winifred Nicholson, Vence, 1927

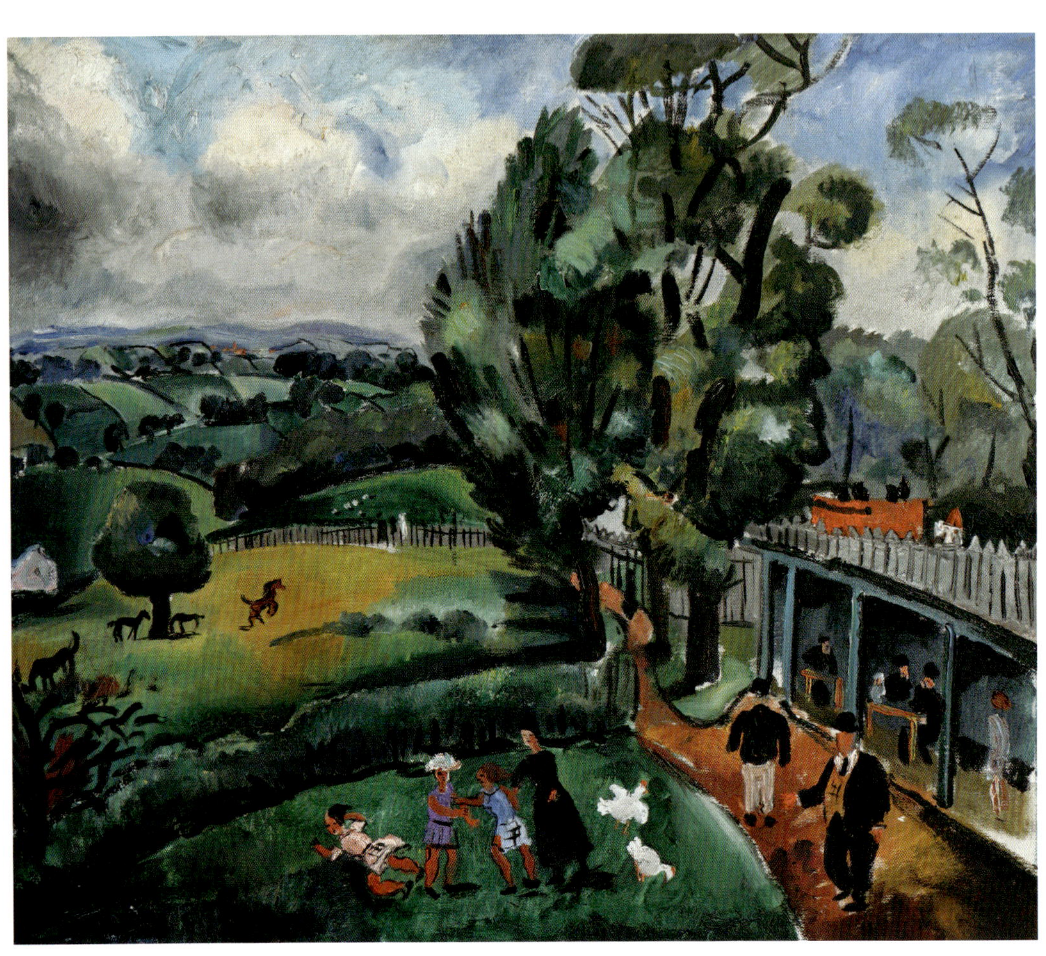

Landscape with Figures, c.1926. Oil on canvas, 500 x 600 mm

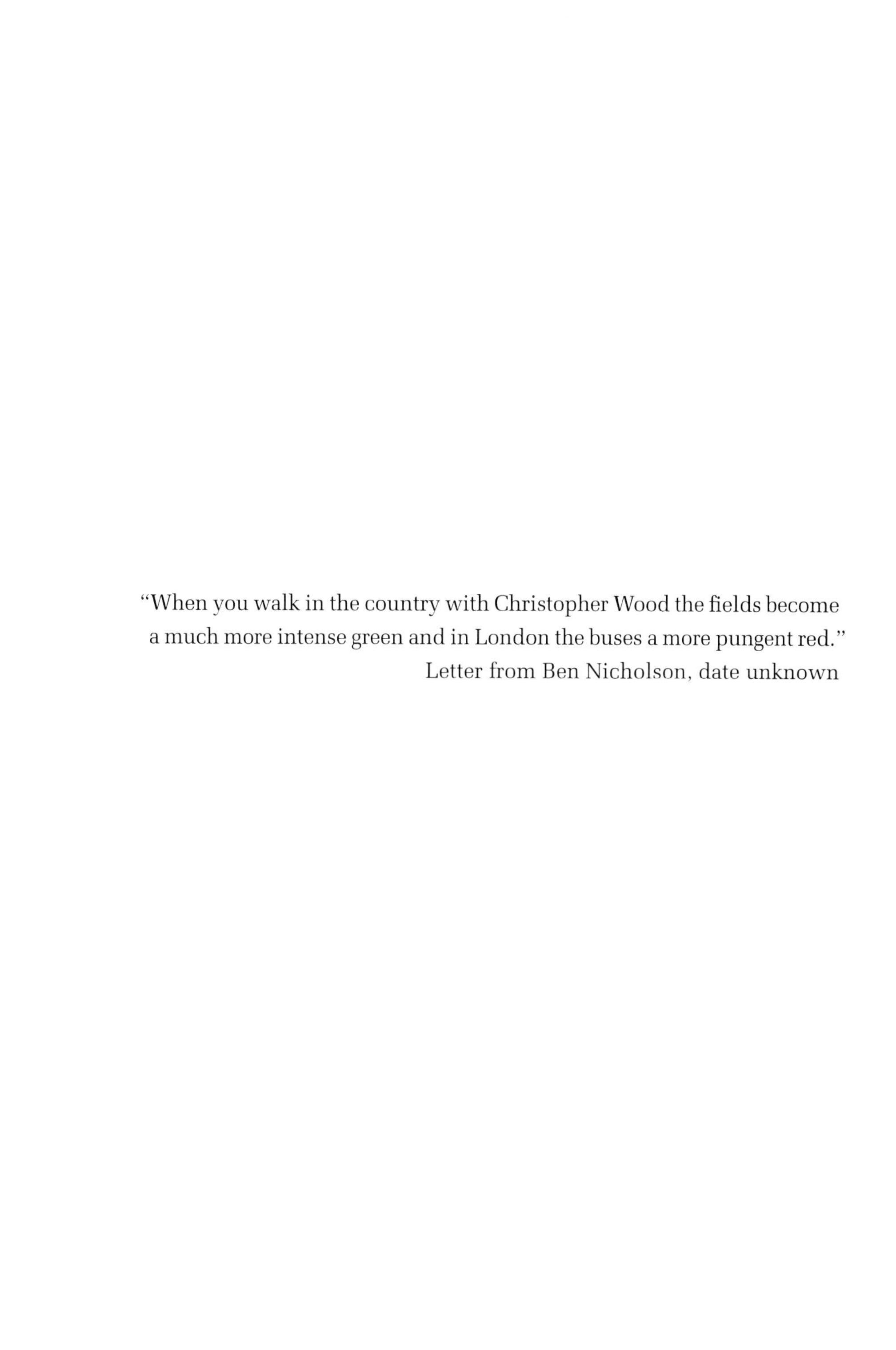

"When you walk in the country with Christopher Wood the fields become a much more intense green and in London the buses a more pungent red."

Letter from Ben Nicholson, date unknown

BETWEEN 1922-29, GANDARILLAS kept a house at 14 Cheyne Walk, a five-story town house in the heart of Chelsea, overlooking the Thames. Wood occupied the top floor as a studio. They used the house on their regular visits to London, having many frequent visitors, entertaining artists, intellectuals and the rich. Regular visitors included Wyndham Lewis, Cedric Morris, Arthur Lett-Haines, the novelist Mary Butts and composer Lord Berners. The Pier Hotel was situated at the end of Cheyne Walk, on the corner with Oakley Street.

In contrast to Paris, the mood in London for most of the Twenties was sombre and inward-looking. The economic toll of the First World War was felt most keenly in the British coal industry. In the space of 7 years, miners' wages had fallen from £6 to £3.90. In May 1926, 1.75 million workers 'from John O'Groats to Lands End' walked out in what was known as the General Strike. Although he visited London relatively frequently, and his financial situation was never stable, Wood remained somewhat sheltered from the economic crisis; in the same month as the General Strike, Gandarillas paid £350 for a new Delage.

Sebastian Faulks described 1920s London as a society "engaged in a battle on all fronts to keep the modern world at bay." Post-war England was deeply suspicious of the ideas circulating on the continent, in art as much as in politics. In France, Picasso's genius was recognised and deferred to; here he was regarded with distaste, except by a handful of critics. The 7&5 Society formed in 1919 to champion traditional, conservative artistic sensibilities. The first exhibition catalogue said, "[we] feel that there has of late been too much pioneering along too many lines in altogether too much of a hurry." Rather than the energetic Vorticists' 'new world order', the decade began with a return to the artistic values of the old guard of Walter Sickert, Augustus John and William Nicholson.

Meeting Picasso brought the limitations of British painting into sharp relief for Wood. But in 1926, Cedric Morris introduced Wood to like-minded young British artists Ben and Winifred Nicholson. Shortly after their meeting, Wood wrote to the Nicholsons "We must make things sit up in England!" At Ben Nicholson's invitation, Wood joined the 7&5 Society, and found himself amongst a stable of forward-thinking, artists that included David Jones, Barbara Hepworth and Henry Moore. Wood developed a close friendship with Ben and Winifred Nicholson. Despite his relative inexperience, Wood was an inspiring painting partner for Nicholson, who understood the significance of the artistic

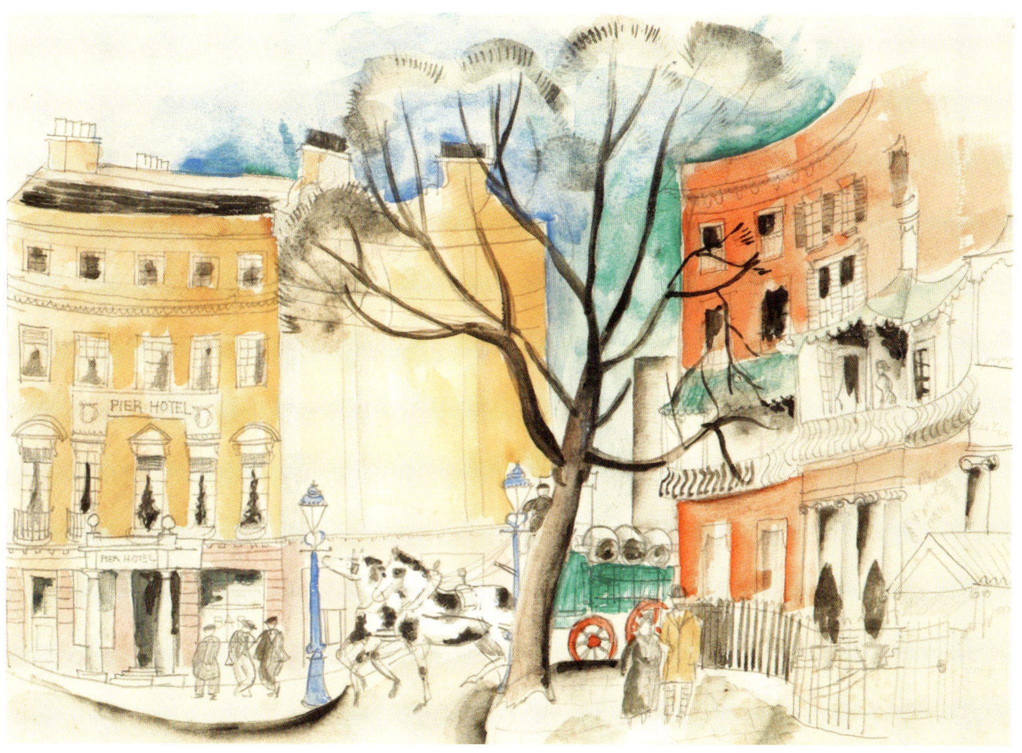

developments in Europe. They shared an artistic vision and helped one another to make their first steps in the art world. Wood took part in various 7&5 exhibitions in London between 1927 and 1930, and when he was offered his first one-man show in Paris in 1930, he invited Ben Nicholson to share it.

It was, however, Winifred Nicholson who perhaps connected most deeply with Wood and best understood his artistic temperament, as her writing about the artist's work reveals. When Wood came to visit their London home, Winifred vividly recalled hearing his voice from upstairs for the first time:

> "I was dressing in a little white bedroom I had in our flat in Chelsea – we were going out to dinner with Jim (Ede) – and somebody was talking with Ben and Cedric down in Ben's studio. I had no idea who it was but they went on talking and talking, he with a voice that moved me strangely."

Pier Hotel, Chelsea, c.1927. Watercolour and graphite on paper, 250 x 350 mm

14 Cheyne Walk

Sunday

Dear Jim

I was sorry not to see you again after that delightful concert but I was obliged to hurry away to an appointment at six o'clock – I will try and ring you up tomorrow and arrange a meeting but I have so little time left and so many things to do in it that if I don't please forgive me as I am now leaving on Tuesday evening instead of Wednesday. It has been a great nuisance to have to rush away like this and was so enjoying London and seeing people that I like. Still I am going to Greece again and to me that country with all its objections is irresistable. I wish to thank you again for all the kind things you have done for me

Letter from Christopher Wood to Jim Ede, undated

which I will never forget and
I hope that I may repay
you for them in some way
one day. I will do anything
I can in my power to help
you if ever there was a
possibility of doing so.
If I dont see you again
goodbye and all my thanks

Ever yr

Kit

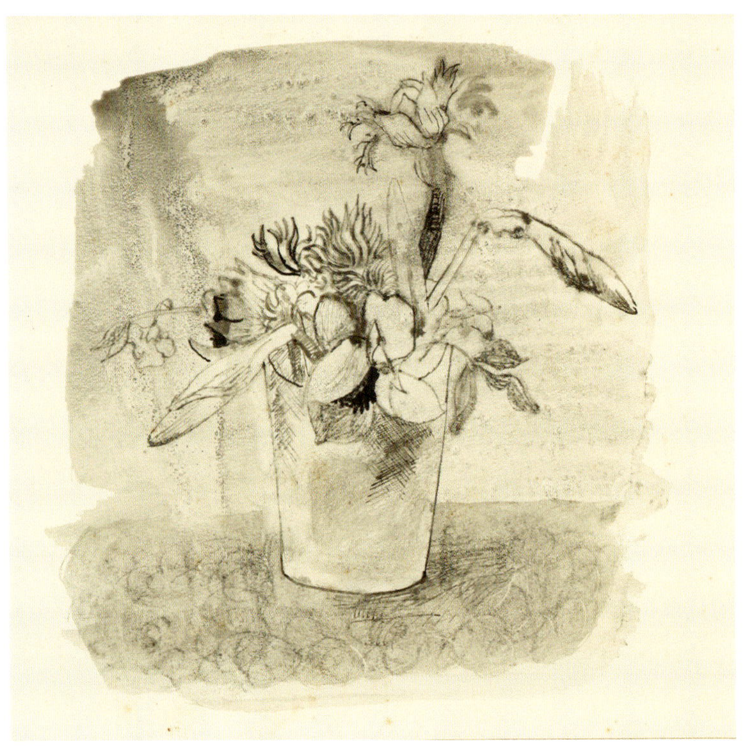

The Nicholsons and Wood formed a close friendship and shared ideas and techniques. Winifred sent Wood flowers to paint in Paris. Wood wrote back:

> "Thank you so much for thinking of me and sending me these flowers. Nothing, I say nothing because I mean nothing, has given me such pleasure as they did arriving as they did and when they did. Only you could have packed them so well and in such a way that they would arrive fresher than they left." Saturday evening, Paris, 1927

Flowers, 1930. Pen and ink and wash on paper, 230 x 240 mm

Flowers (detail), 1930. Oil on board, 330 x 400 mm

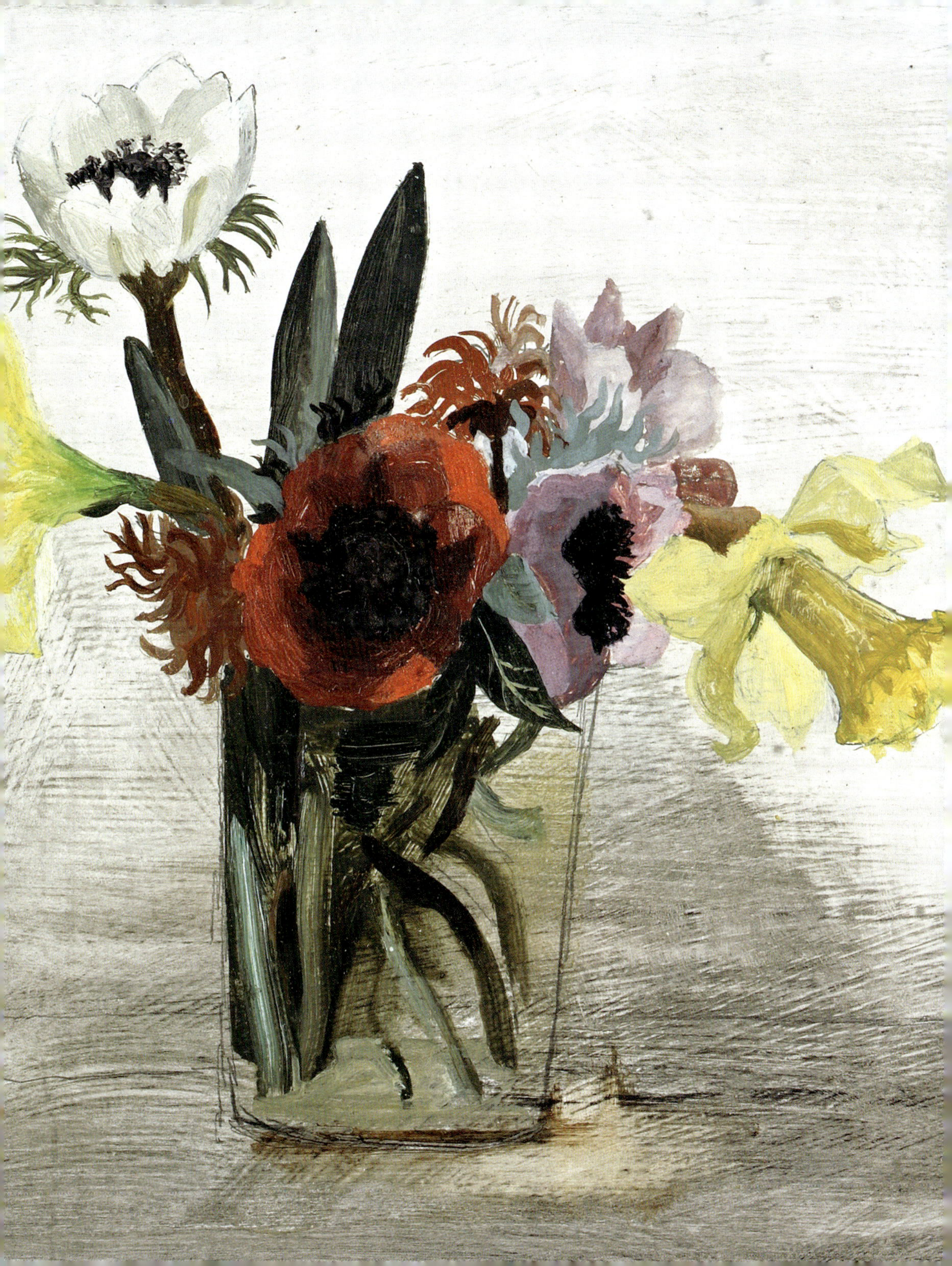

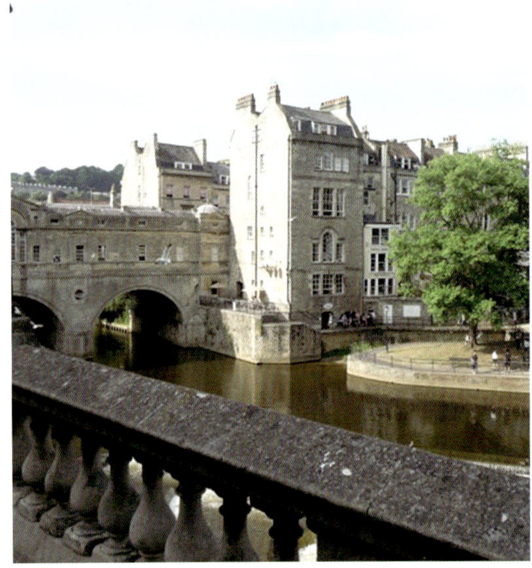

The collection includes two drawings made in Bath, drawn from the same position on the first floor balcony of the Empire Hotel. The first is a view of Pulteney Bridge over the River Avon; the second depicts a view over the river towards the cricket pitch and Bathwick Hill.

The Empire Hotel, Bath, photograph by Anthony Hepworth, 2013

Houses and River, Bath, c.1927. Graphite on paper, 260 x 340 mm

Landscape, c.1927. Graphite on paper, 260 x 340 mm

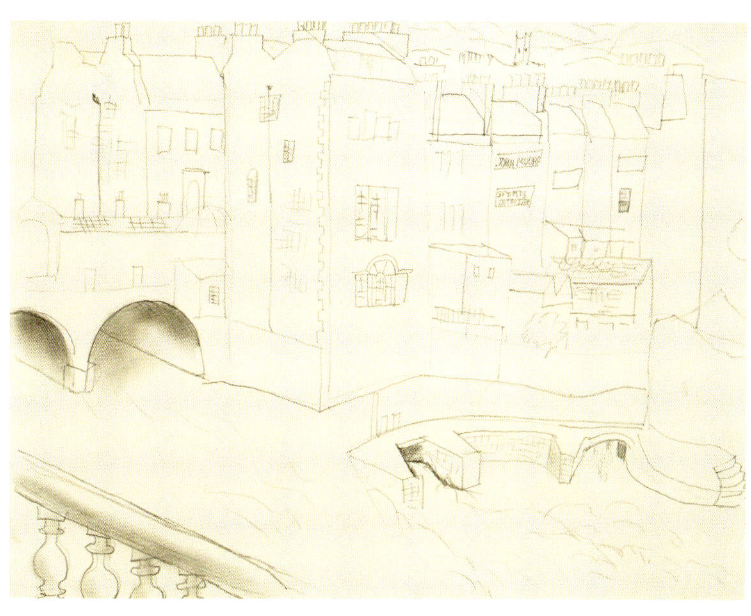

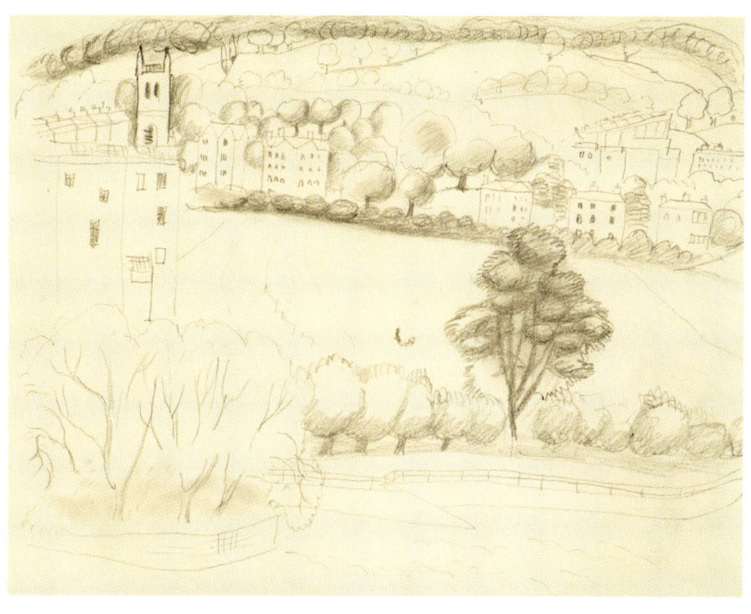

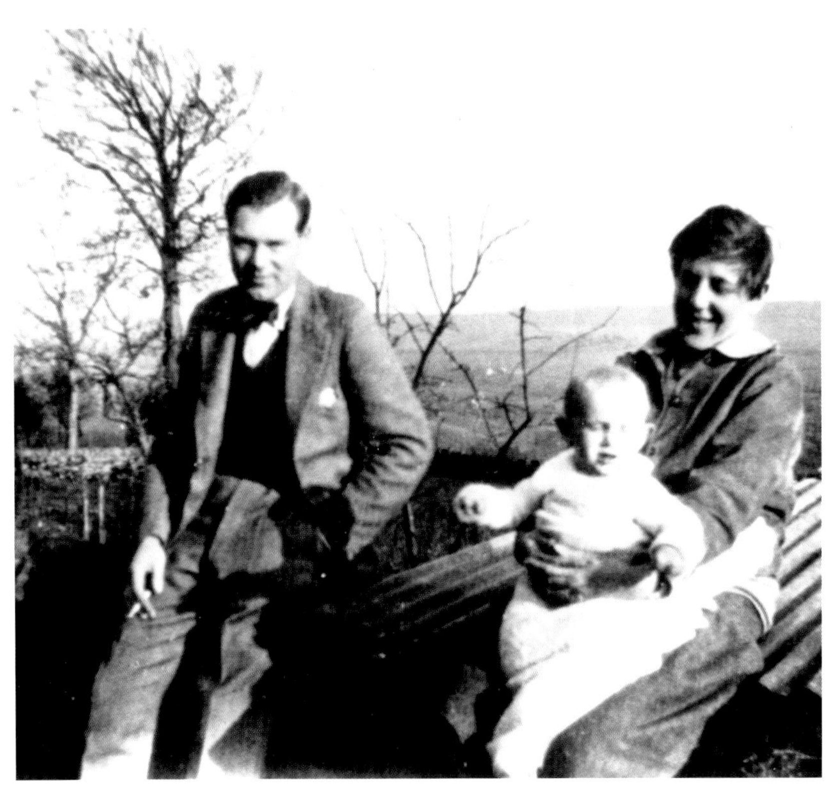

Christopher Wood and Winifred Nicholson with baby, c.1925-1930

IN MARCH 1928 THE NICHOLSONS invited Wood to Bankshead, their Cumberland home, for what turned out to be an intense period of activity for all three artists. Winifred later wrote:

> "His arrival was like a meteor. The wild country delighted him. The dark forests took on mystery and magic as he looked on them, moved in spirit with the impetuosity of the brown river that runs, carving its course through Coombe Crags. We all three painted and thought of nothing else. Inspiration ran high and flew backwards and forwards from one to the other."
>
> Nicholson, Winifred, 'Blue was his Colour', *Unknown Colour: Paintings, Letters, Writings by Winifred Nicholson*, ed. Andrew Nicholson, London: Faber and Faber, 1987, p. 86

Wood was inspired by the stark landscape of Cumberland and the simple married life of Ben and Winifred. He wrote:

> "Bankshead is the painter's life, and if I could find a little peace of mind I am absolutely on the verge of the real thing after what I saw and learnt at Bankshead."
>
> Letter from Christopher Wood to Ben and Winifred Nicholson, undated, c.1928

During his visit, and no doubt inspired by the relative austerity of the Nicholsons' lifestyle, Wood tried to wean himself off opium, but resumed the habit when he returned to Paris.

> "Ben and Kit had made friends with a friendship and fellowship in their work which brought the very best of them to flowering point – It was great fun to see – the zest and vitality and life in it meant everything to us all."
>
> Letter from Winifred Nicholson to Frosca Munster, undated, c.1930

Back in Paris, Wood met Frosca Munster, a Russian émigré who had managed to bring much of her wealth out of Russia. She had been married, and although part of the same social world as Wood, she was also sceptical of it. Her reserve and gentle nature reminded him of Winifred Nicholson. They formed an attachment quickly, with Frosca often accompanying Wood on painting trips.

Bankshead.

Dear Jim

I shall be in London Thursday evening. Would you dine with me – I'm going to Paris on Friday morning for a bit so will stay the night at the Grosvenor Hotel. Drop me a line if this suits and pick me up there about 7.30

I long to hear of your French visit & to see you again –

Yrs

Kit –

Will give you the Bankshead news.

Letter from Christopher Wood to Jim Ede, undated

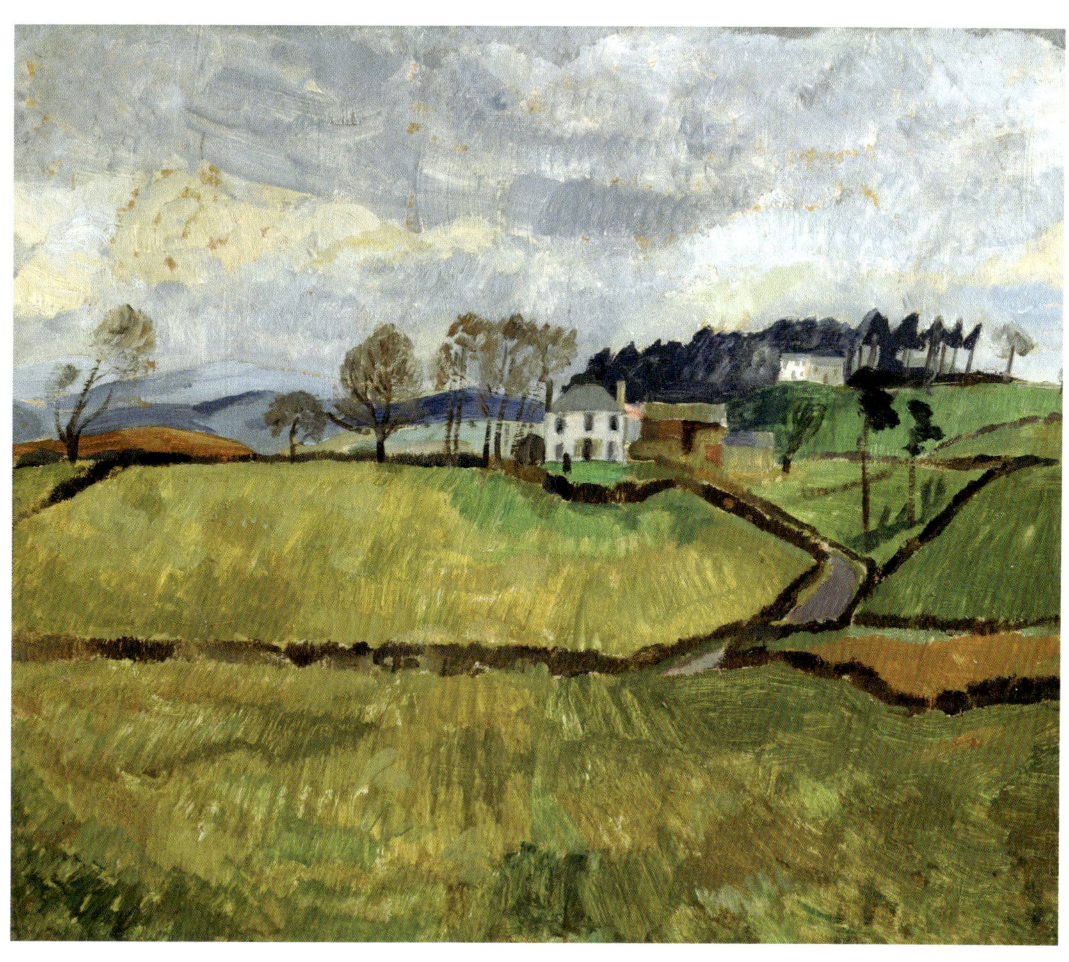

Cumberland Landscape (Northrigg Hill), 1928. Oil on board, 510 x 605 mm
Gift of Ruth and Paul Dillon, 2010

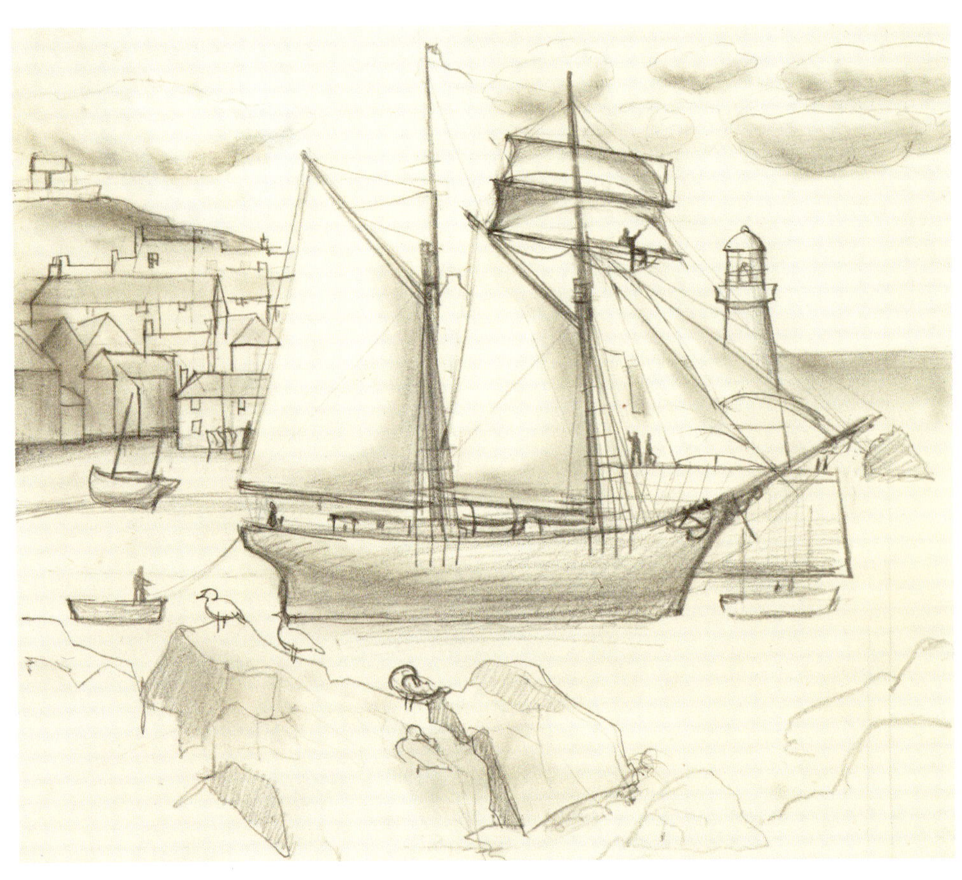

Ship in Harbour, 1928. Graphite on paper, 260 x 300 mm
Inscribed in Ede's hand "Christopher Wood / Ship (for Lord Berners)"

Later that summer, Wood returned to Cornwall with the Nicholsons, staying first in Feock, then in St Ives, where Frosca joined them. In August, Ben and Kit took a day trip to St Ives and made their legendary 'discovery' of the primitive painter, Alfred Wallis. It was a critical turning point for Wood. When Frosca and the Nicholsons left, he stayed on alone in St Ives until late November. He had found his subject: the wild sea and wide horizons, the ancient coast and the plain, spiritual life of the seafaring community, his mother's ancestors; the sailing boats with their colourful sails and sparkling fish on the quayside. He wrote:

> "I seem to live on the very edge of the world. But what an edge it is. I love this place and could stay here forever."
>
> Letter from Christopher Wood to Winifred, Ben and Jake Nicholson, St Ives, undated

This painting depicts St Ives harbour, although from a less familiar viewpoint, at the end of the old sea wall on the western edge of the bay. Wood wrote to the Nicholsons:

> "I like the port from the other side with Church and hills behind – its all brown and beige grey with startling white windows in all the houses the hills are straight and hard and in the tops are windswept trees and telegraph poles. St Ives is on the edge of Europe and the first English rebuff to those coming from distant parts."
>
> Letter from Christopher Wood to Winifred, Ben and Jake Nicholson, St Ives, undated

> "the coastland is arid with huge rocks and towering black cliffs, and little coves and creeks with the greenest water you ever saw, with little white cottages clinging like wild flowers to the rocks."
>
> Letter from Christopher Wood to Clare Wood, undated

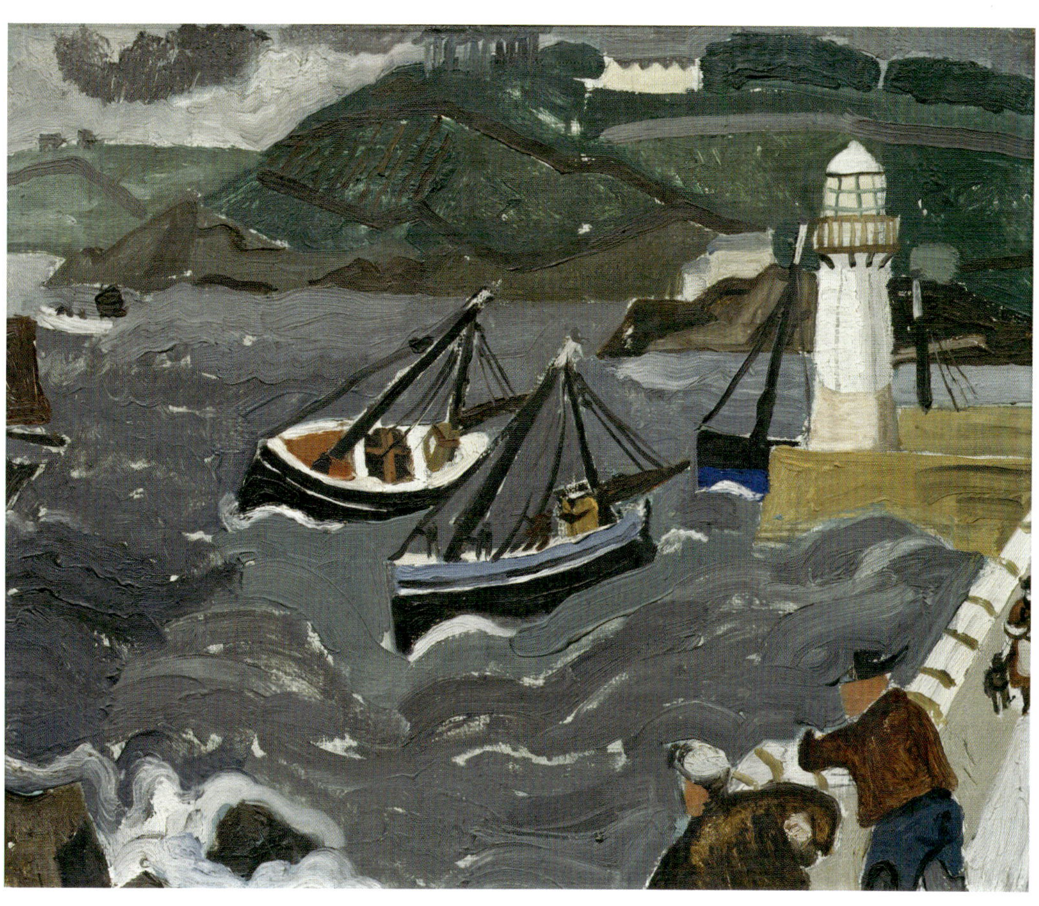

Harbour in the Hills, 1930. Oil on canvas, 359 x 436 mm
Courtesy of the University of Essex

Wood and the Nicholsons were inspired by Wallis' unselfconscious technique, and they also picked up a few techniques from the old fisherman. One such technique was the use of a white gesso ground – under the trade name of Coverine – which all three would overlay and scrape down or incise, to stress surface and texture and show the working processes. Winifred wrote of painting together in Cornwall in 1928, "We painted most of our pictures this summer on coverine. It was his idea. It dries fast. You can put it over old pictures." (Winifred Nicholson, 'Blue was his Colour', p.93). In effect, this echoed Wallis' use of his supports and emphasised the objecthood of the painting. When the Nicholsons had returned to London, Wood wrote to Winifred:

> "What did Jim think of Admiral Wallis – I often see. Took him some baccy and a few papers last evening ... more and more influencé de Wallis and not a bad master though, he and Picasso both mix their colours on box lids!"
>
> Letter from Christopher Wood to Winifred Nicholson, 1928

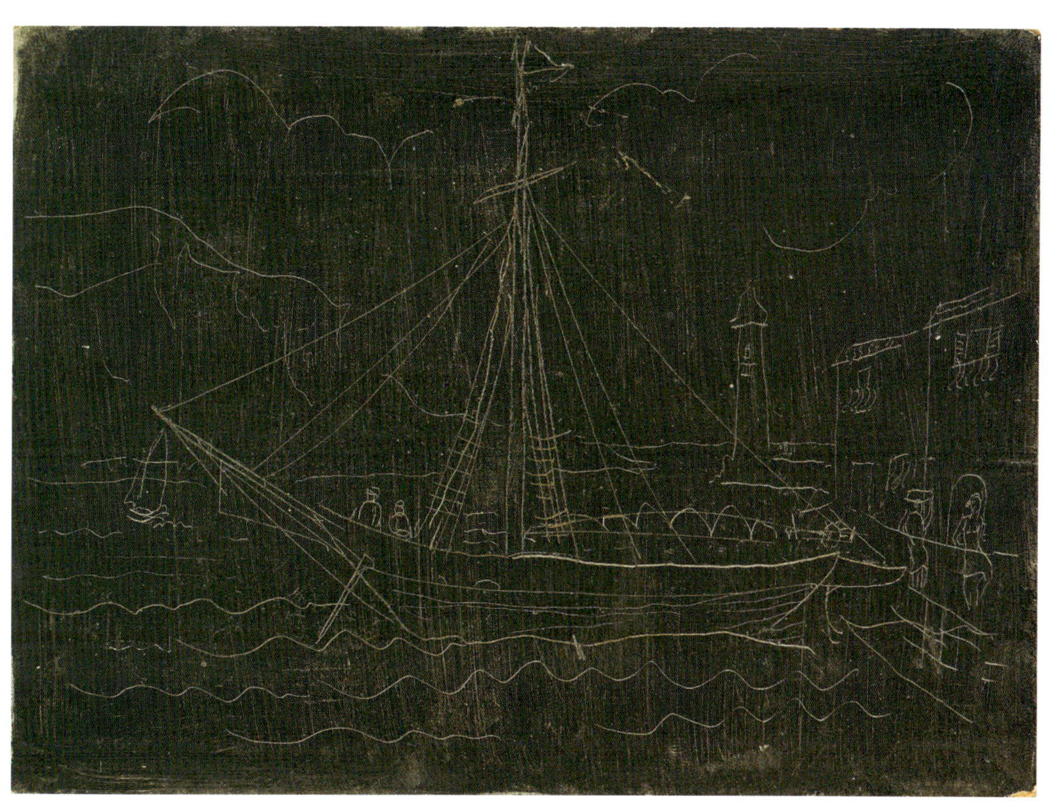

Ship in Harbour, 1928. Incised on brown washed board, 160 x 220 mm

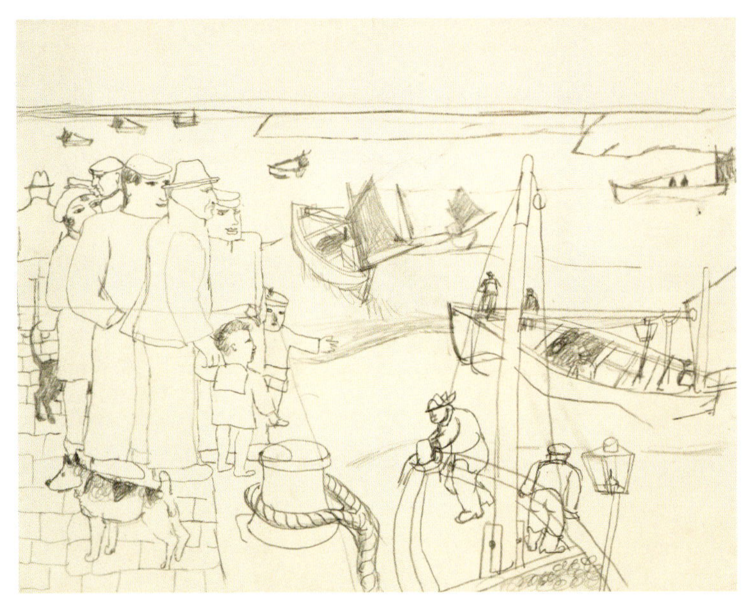

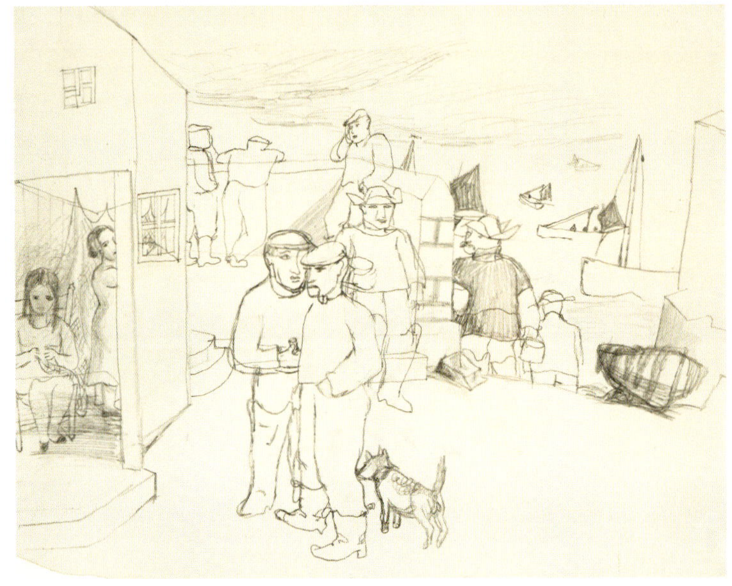

IN DECEMBER 1928, WOOD RETURNED TO PARIS and moved in with Frosca Munster. But his internal compass had shifted, and at the end of January 1929, Wood set himself up in a small house at 3 Minton Place, back in London. Frosca stayed with him here while he prepared for a 7&5 show at Tooth's Gallery in March. Wood and Nicholson included three works by Wallis in this exhibition, and some critics felt that Wallis' genuine naïveté cast their work in an unfavourable light. The experience was a disappointment for Wood and in April, he went with Frosca to Dieppe. She reported:

> "Kit is working like a mad thing. He never puts down his paint brush for a second … never has there been such a profusion of pictures."
>
> Letter from Frosca Munster to Ben and Winifred Nicholson, 1929

Wood wrote a postcard from Dieppe to the Nicholsons:

> "It is a bit like B'head as far as temperature is concerned but lacks the nice quiet places and wild distances. Otherwise it is just what I like not too much of anything lovely, houses port cliffs with green grass and the kind of boats that Mr Wallis used to sail in."
>
> Dieppe, 1929

St. Ives, c.1928. Graphite on paper, 350 x 450 mm
Gift of Ben Nicholson

Fishermen and Boats, 1928. Graphite on paper, 350 x 450 mm

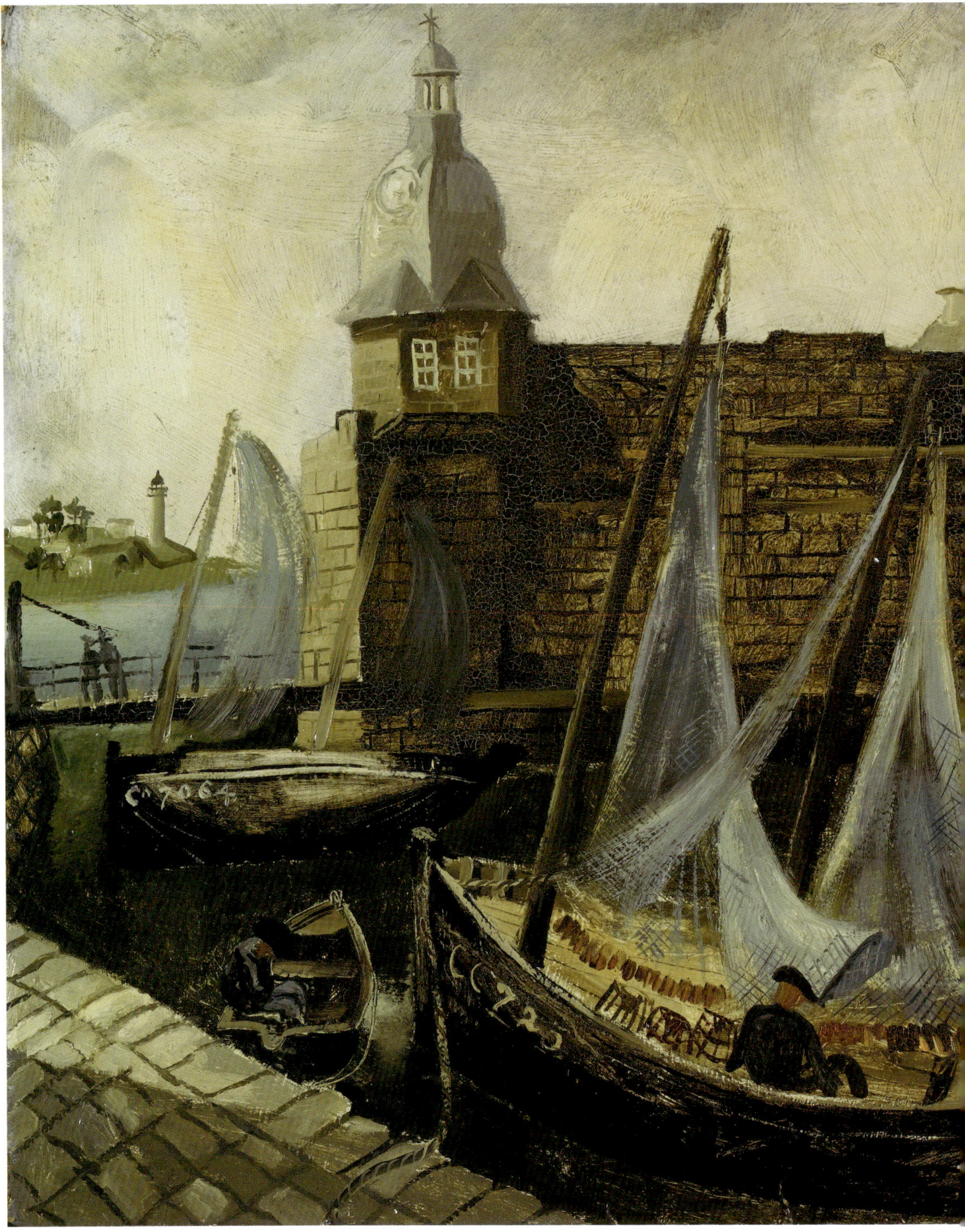

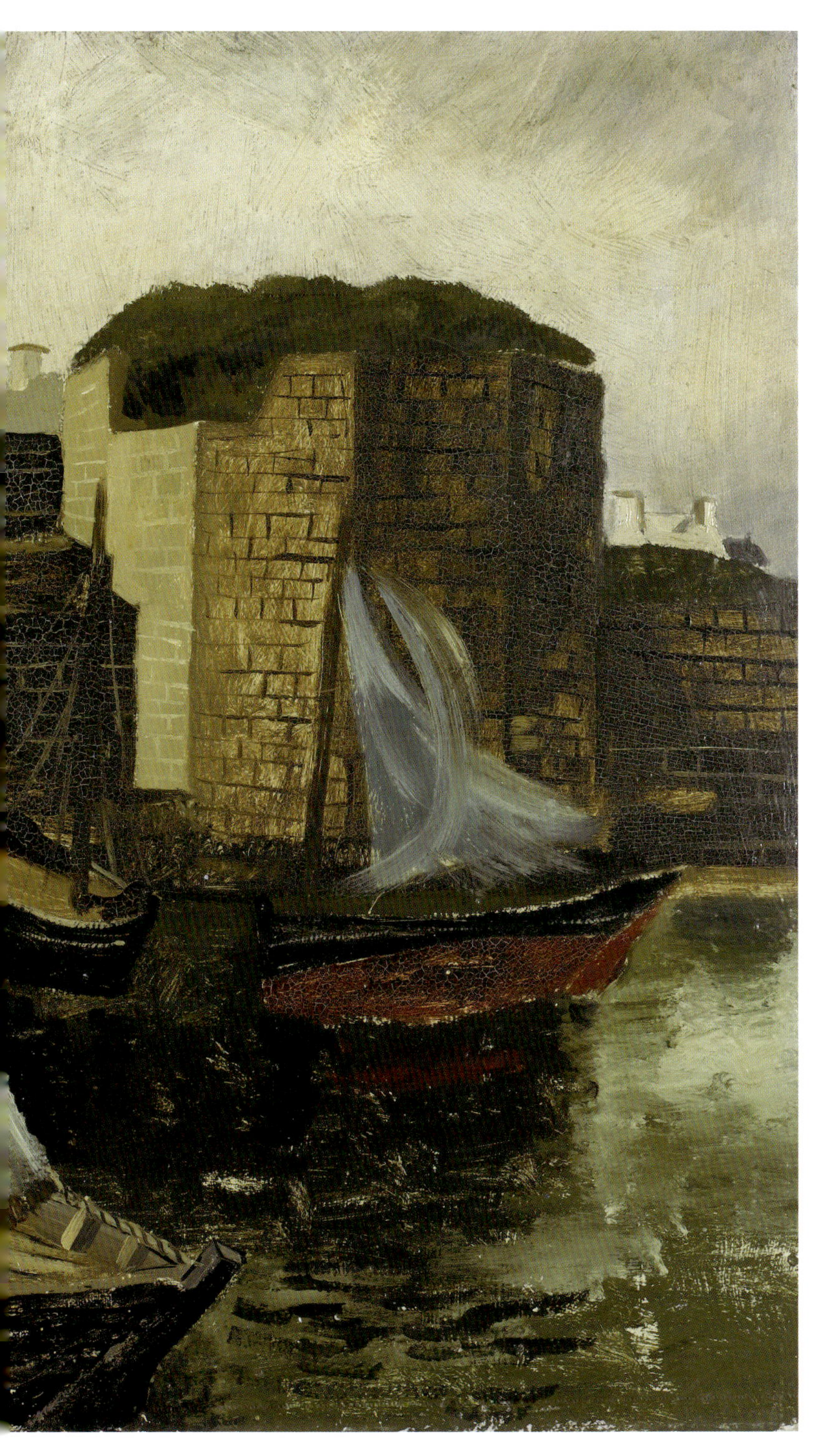

La Ville-Close, Concarneau, Brittany, 1930
Oil on board, 560 x 808 mm
Courtesy of the Fitzwilliam Museum

They returned briefly to Paris in May, which is probably when Wood painted the portrait of Jeanne Bourgoint; in July Wood made another trip to Brittany, this time starting in Dinard before visiting St Malo, St Servan and Douarnenez, arriving in Tréboul in August. Wood stayed there until October. Tréboul was a small fishing village on the western side of a long sea inlet whose eastern side was occupied by the commercial port of Douarnenez. In 1929, the villagers put out their fishing boats from a tiny harbour and still wore the traditional Breton dress they had worn for centuries. Wood wrote to his mother:

> "I sit on the green grass banks above the sea each evening which becomes like a lake, pale grey blue like milk and lovely ivory-coloured sailing ships go past very slowly ... I can't tell you the beauty of this place with dark fir trees and the little white houses like jewels, the curious faces of the people like Holbein's drawings, there is such dignity and compactness about everything."

Francis Rose recalled the summer of 1929:

> "Kit, from a fishing boat, painted pictures of other fishing boats. He used Ripoline house paint, thinned with turpentine, and his colours were clear and pure. No real sail held as much of the brown and orange of a sun-lit sail as did those of his paintings ... His lobster baskets were as wet in colour and as well drawn in pattern as the real ones, and there was never a suspicion of the decorative in his work."

On his return to Paris, Wood was offered a one-man show the following May at the Georges Bernheim Gallery. His was an important gallery on the rue du Faubourg St Honoré, and this show would make him the first English artist to be exhibited in Paris since Whistler. Boris Kochno, who was by then running the Ballets Russes, also commissioned Wood to design the scenery for a revue entitled *Luna Park*, which was to open in March 1930. Despite these promising opportunities, Wood was in financial difficulties. The bailiffs seized his house in Minton Place on 25 October 1929, the day after the collapse of the New York Stock Exchange on Black Thursday. Most of Wood's rich friends in Paris, including Gandarillas and his aunt, were ruined. On Christmas Eve, Jeanne Bourgoint died of barbiturate poisoning, just months after the publication of *Les Enfants Terribles*. Wood worked hard on the designs for *Luna Park* through January, then went to Mousehole in Cornwall to paint more work for the Bernheim show. Meanwhile Bernheim found him a house in Paris where he could continue to work quietly. Wood sold 11 paintings from the show to Lucy Wertheim, a London collector and dealer, who offered him a show in London in October. He left Paris in early June to return to Tréboul.

DURING HIS LAST STAY IN TRÉBOUL Wood worked feverishly, painting more than forty paintings in as many days. He stayed in the Hôtel Ty-Mad, a far cry from the luxurious establishments he'd frequented with Gandarillas. Fellow residents included the poet Max Jacob and English artist Francis Rose. He painted into the night, and smoked opium to sustain the creative process. His supplies of opium didn't match his need for it and he began to smoke and even eat the 'dross' – the residue left in the pipe after the smoker has inhaled. His misuse of opium began to have psychological side effects, but Wood was in a desperate hurry to paint as much as he could while he could. Wood was also increasingly anxious to earn enough money to support himself and marry Frosca; he was acutely aware that his lack of financial resources was an obstacle. Wood returned to Paris in late July, where he painted *Tiger and Arc de Triomphe* and *Zebra with Parachute*.

On 19 August 1930, Wood boarded a train from Paris to Le Havre with three large packages of paintings, two suitcases, his opium pipe and a revolver. He took a boat to Southampton, stopping overnight on the Isle of Wight. On the crossing, Wood began to suspect he was being followed, and threw his opium pipe overboard.

Witnesses at the time have given accounts which suggest that he was becoming increasingly paranoid as he made his way from the Isle of Wight to Salisbury to meet his mother and sister for lunch on 21 August. After what they later recalled as a pleasant and uneventful lunch, they dropped him off at Salisbury station. At 2.10pm, as the Atlantic Coast Express was pulling into the station, Wood jumped in front of the train.

His death was officially reported as accidental, although events suggest it was suicide. Jim Ede and the Nicholsons also found it difficult to believe this was the case. They hired a private investigator to retrace his movements over his last few days in the hope that they might uncover new evidence to explain the puzzle of their friend's death, but nothing conclusive was ever established.

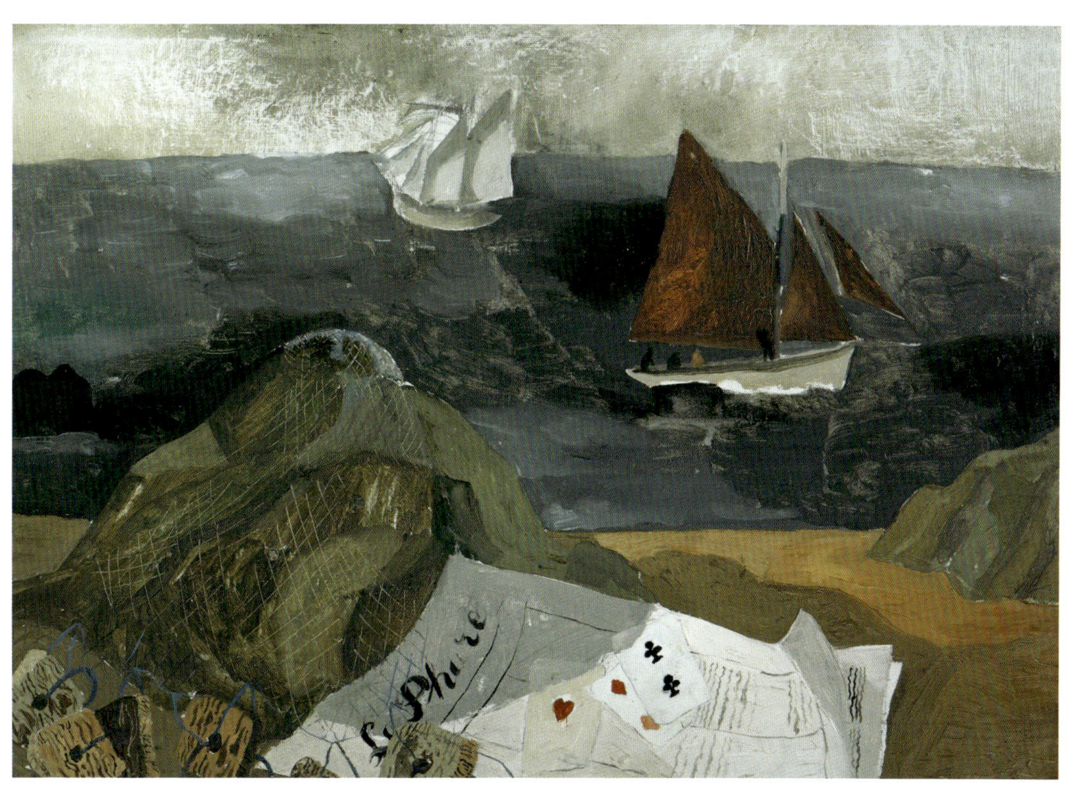

Le Phare, 1929. Oil on board, 535 x 790 mm
Inscription "Bought for £12 / Property of HS Ede"

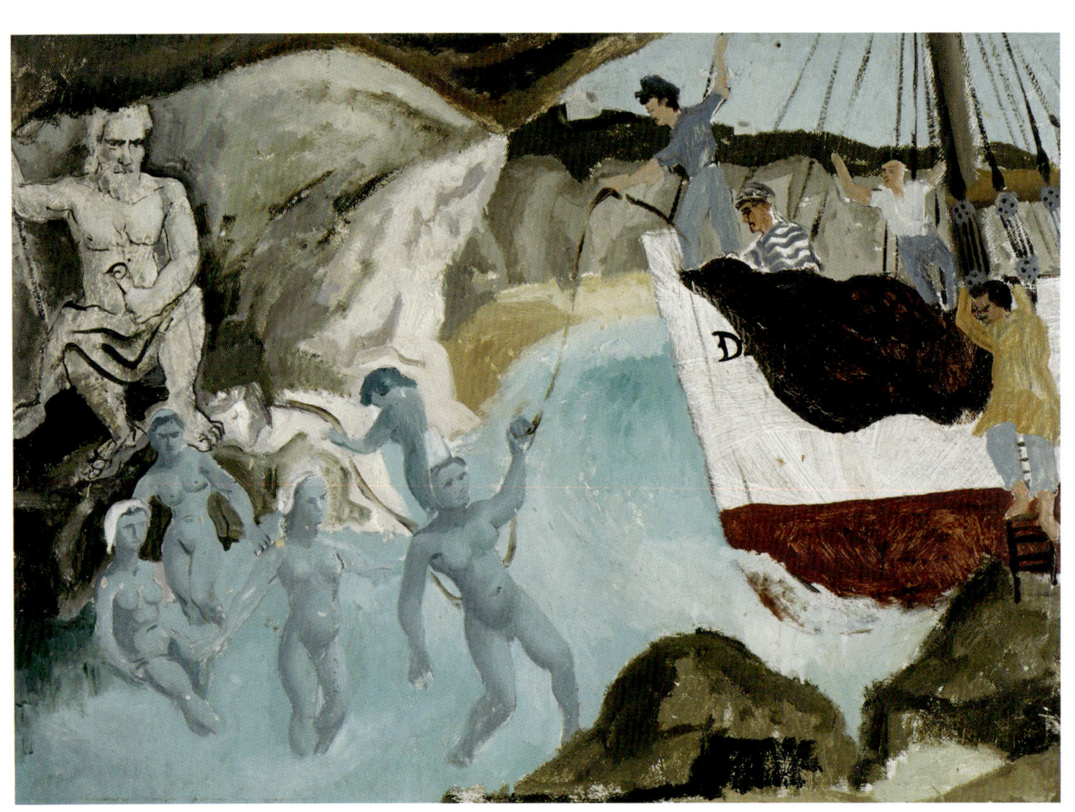

Ulysses and the Sirens (or Mermaids), 1929. Oil on hardboard, 550 x 790 mm

"My life is like the time between sleeping and awakening in the morning."

Letter from Christopher Wood
to Winifred Nicholson, Paris, 12 June 1928

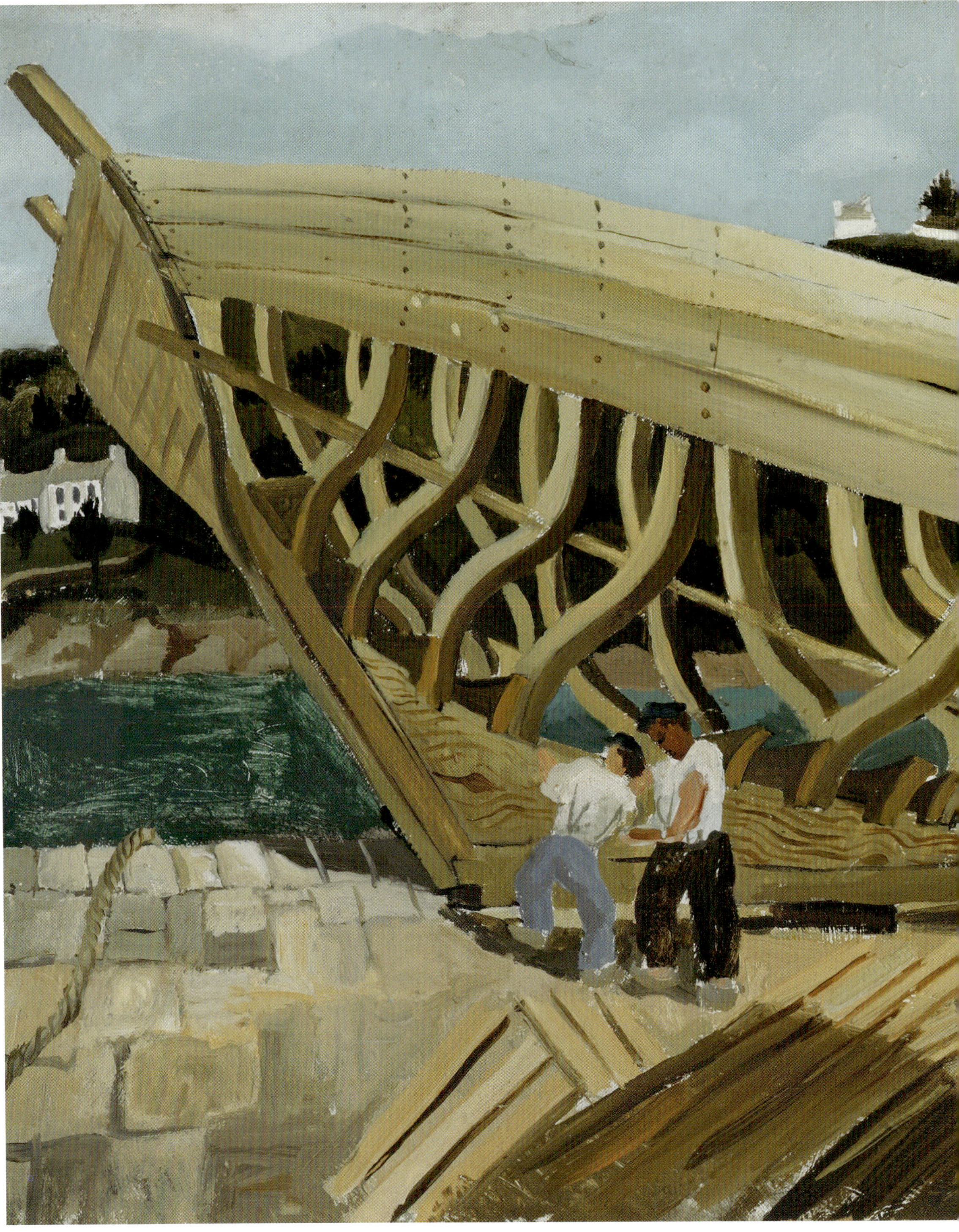

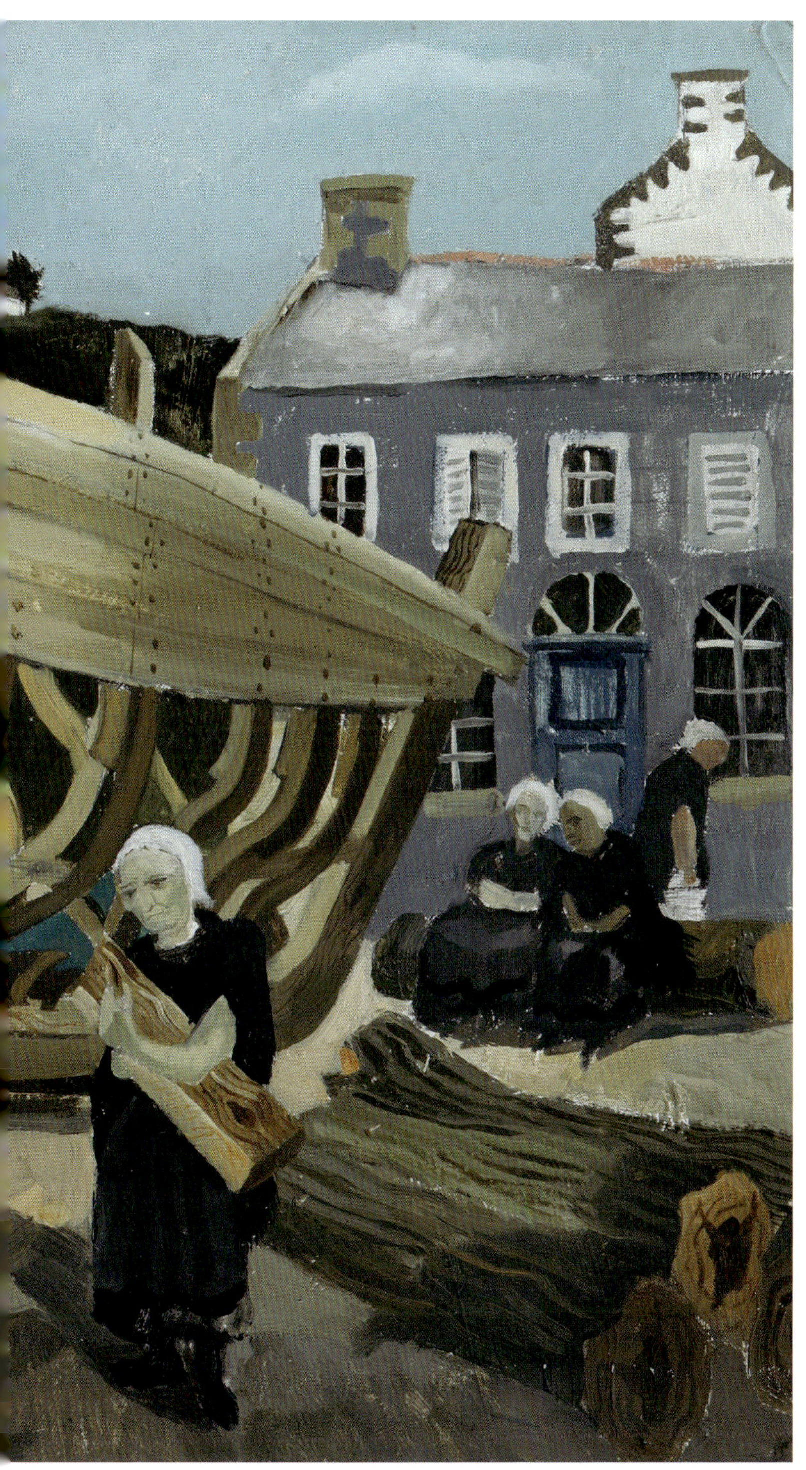

Building the Boat, Tréboul, depicts the boat builders in Place de l'Enfer, just a short walk from the small village of Tréboul, in Douarnenez. It was an important port for sardine fishing and is still a centre for boat building and repair work today.

Building the Boat, Tréboul, 1930
Oil on board, 560 x 810 mm

CHRISTOPHER WOOD IN BRITTANY

A Souvenir by Max Jacob

"The Bretons", he used to say, "make one believe in Paradise." Kit got on with them well and understood them because he was like them himself. Always slightly sad, even when making fun, reserved until he made friends, he did not make friends easily. But he had that particular genius which is the capacity to understand the world before having lived in it. What Kit Wood also had in common with the Bretons was their tact. He was as strong as an ox ... completely honest, not ashamed to ask forgiveness for any hurt he had unwittingly caused. He also had the dignity of nobility in common with the Bretons ... the bearing of a saint who does not need to pray because of his faith.

I can remember the humble and pious Breton women who used to wait upon us at the Pension Cariou drying their tears on their aprons at the news of his death, and I know without doubt they were praying for his soul.

Under the trees and near the rocks by the bay of Douarnenez, Kit lived for two months; his last, alas! Neither the October storms nor the horrible recollection of his death could deter me from returning there. The wind was howling against the door of his room. I did not dare enter nor cross the threshold which now seemed like a tomb... this landing which used to ring with our laughter! There on the table could no longer be seen the wet canvases, the brushes and pots of paint. No longer on top of the high wardrobe were the paintings which he had just completed in the space of a few hours with such vigour and which he surveyed with apprehension and maybe melancholy. I shall never see again the larch tree below his window hiding the sea and the minute chapel which he loved to paint ... "You hear the birds singing in your tree," was said by one of the rare poets who looked at this painting. Kit was so much a poet himself and so humble that he was touched by the beauty of the image.

To-day the sea is green and the sky is black. Kit saw Finisterre through the eyes of his own country, the country of the Bronte sisters. He painted that particular autumn with the brush of a master.

There were some days, the nights before the dawn, his voice seemed to awaken me... his very soul was present ... his philosophy, his ingenuousness and humour came flashing back to me. He seemed to put his hand upon my shoulder. May God take care of his soul ... this man who in a way was heroic, a child who was curious of everything.

Published in Newton, Eric, *Christopher Wood: His Life and Work*, London: Redfern Gallery, 1959, p.19

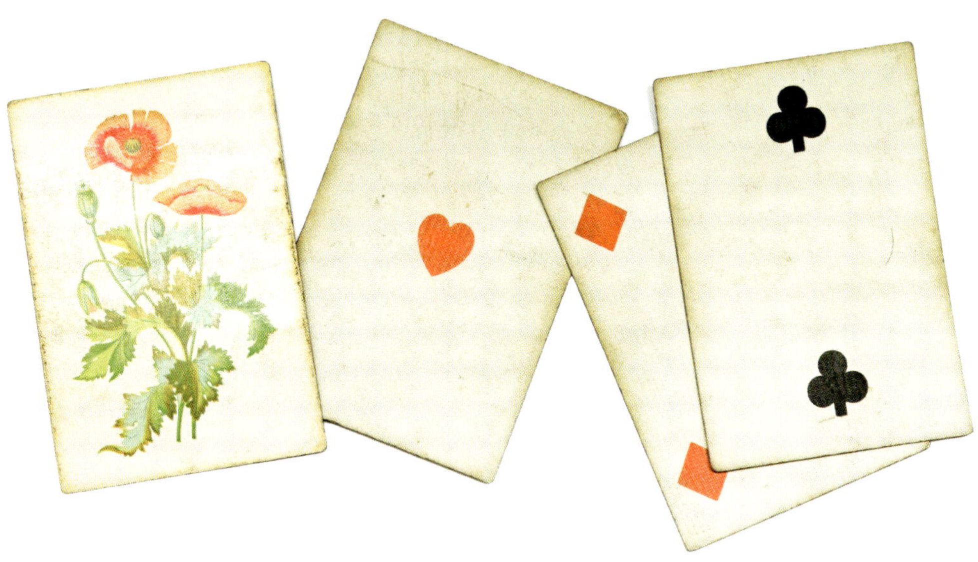

Christopher Wood's playing cards
Manufactured by De La Rue, early 20th century

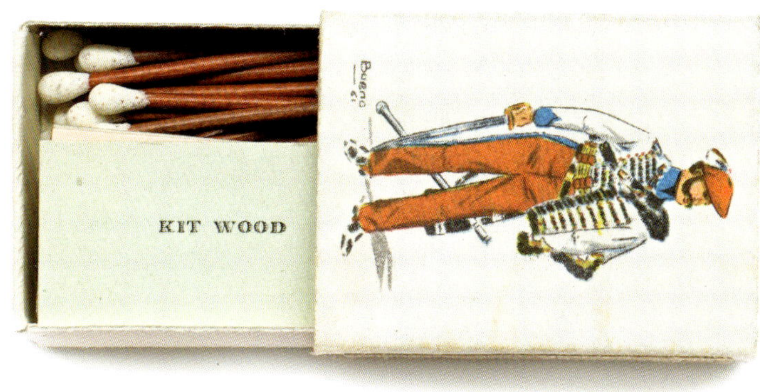

Christopher Wood's calling cards and matchbox

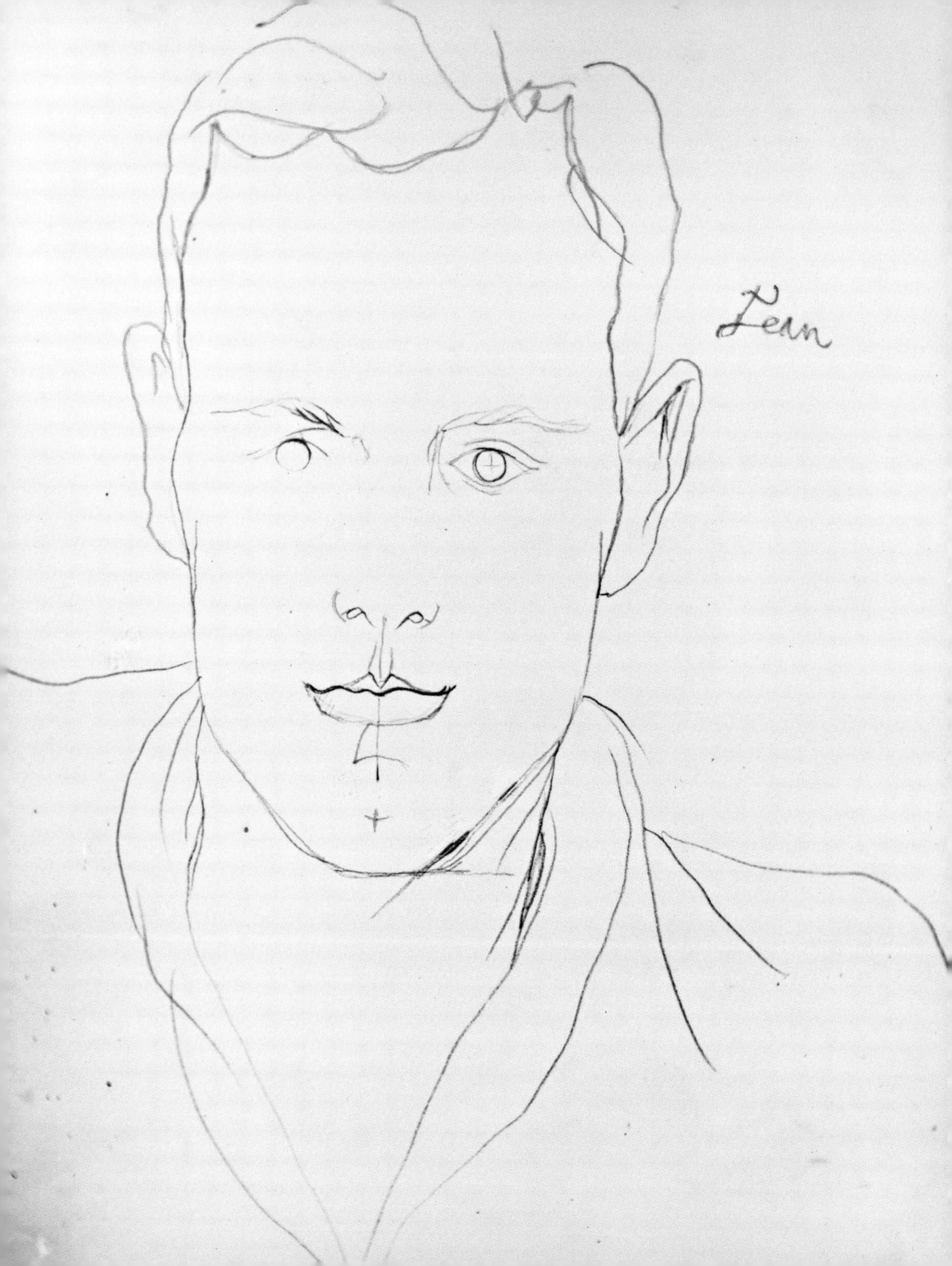
Jean

CHRISTOPHER WOOD

by John Piper

Christopher Wood was essentially a 'contemporary' painter. He always worked in, and did something towards determining, an idiom which belonged entirely to his own day. He widened its scope, and that is a lot to be able to say of any painter who died at the age of twenty-nine. Whether or not he would have achieved a still riper expression had he lived to paint in his maturity – a tantalising problem – is of no consequence in considering the fine quality of the work he actually produced. Possibly he would not have gone much further, for reasons I shall touch on later. From the time when he first began painting seriously (he worked in a City office after leaving school) he seems to have struck straight at the roots of the modern problems – problems that resolved themselves for him into something like this: "How can I paint a picture which, while being a living entity by itself, shall also be an expression of those feelings I experience in the face of nature and humanity?" In fact, his problem, like that of so many, perhaps of all, good painters was one of creating a parallel to visual facts, and not an imitation. He was never a mere imitator of nature or of other art, and his paintings always have a distinguished quality, the result of a well-used and well-cherished vision and a fine unity of purpose. They are vigorous, but they are subtle, and, above all, they are human. He was an abstract painter in that he ignored many truths for the sake of expressing a few well, but his thrilled interest in his subjects ruled out any possibility of his pictures being abstract in the emotionally-cold sense. They are the products of genuine, often fleeting, and always poignant reactions.

The Memorial Exhibition now open at Lefevre Gallery shows his art at the climax it reached just before his death in 1930. The excited vigour which his work always had is here sustained longer than in his earlier paintings, so that his characterisation of a subject is realised more subtly. His technique was always his servant. He never seems to have painted dully in order to master a technique. At any rate, such a process never shows itself in his exhibited work. He was a

left: Drawing of Christopher Wood by Jean Cocteau, undated

gifted draughtsman in that his feelings were strong enough to demand expression, and the means of expression was always at hand, which is saying much the same thing, and which is all that the much-misued work 'gifted' can mean. In other words, he never stated his feelings in a fumbling or inadequate manner. They were too exciting for that, and carried all before them. His boats plunging in dark-watered harbours or idling in creeks seem to have seen with new eyes and their significance seems to have awakened new feelings. These are pictures which live by themselves, even when unrelated to their subjects or the feelings that prompted them, unlike those slices of the artist's life which constitute rather a depressing section of modern art. Nor had Christopher Wood a vision of that naïve order, charming in its childlike simplicity, that some critics have too hastily suggested. It was rich in its grasp of essentials, and in the warmth of humanity that nourished it. This grasp of essentials was important in giving body and life to a naturally vigorous handling. Wood's obvious love of baroque decoration, for instance, is never allowed too free a play: it is always nicely related to a mass, which it both decorates and enlivens. His art in one of its most important phases is represented by the portrait of Max Jacob in the Exhibition, lent by the Luxembourg Gallery. His sense of characterising a subject perfectly, and of giving a picture a life of its own as well, have achieved a fine result. It is a good portrait, but it is also a very good picture.

In his preface to the catalogue Mr. H. S. Ede likens Christopher Wood to Constable in that "his pictures have some of the direct response found in early Constables, that very English quality which makes of a painting the spiritual realisations, profoundly significant, of homely things". And indeed, though owing a great deal to the liberating forces of modern French art, he was a very English painter. "Early Constables", says Mr. Ede: and quite justly so, for Constable later grew in stature as a painter so as to realise those still richer dreams of a spiritually experienced man which Christopher Wood died too young to contemplate. What he would have achieved must remain in doubt. When he died he was more than a promising painter, and it is possible that he had already realised himself more or less fully. Whether or not his art would have weathered the storms of a new and even more important spiritual growth we shall never know, but it is tenable that all young artists who are vital and sincere come to a stage when their emotional response to reality suffers a change involving a partial spiritual death; that the re-growth is a slow and tortuous process, and that many artists have deliberately maimed their potential genius by attempting to withstand this displacement of their early powers – powers which are at their height in late adolescence and early manhood, the more so then because a technique has begun to form itself into an adequate vehicle of expression. It is arguable that a poet such as Rupert Brooke and a painter such as Christopher Wood (to keep only to our own days) died at the critical stage.

Published in *The Listener,* 'Weekly Notes on Art', 20 April 1932 pp. 571-2

CHRONOLOGY

1901 John Christopher Wood was born in Knowlsey, Liverpool on 7 April, to Dr Lucius and Clare Wood.

1907 - 15 Wood was educated at Freshfield Preparatory School and Marlborough College, Wiltshire.

1915 Wood contracted polio and septicaemia and was nursed at home by Clare Wood from 1916-1918. Wood recovered but was left with a permanent limp.

1918 - 19 Studied medicine at Malvern College for one term, then enrolled at Liverpool University to study architecture. Left before completing his first year.

1920 Moved to London. Wood took a job as an apprentice to a fruit farmer. Introduced to art collector Alphonse Kahn by Augustus John. Kahn invited him to Paris.

1921 Wood stayed with Kahn in the Bois de Boulogne in 16th arrondisement and enrolled at the Académie Julian. Through Kahn, Wood met Chilean diplomat, Antonio de Gandarillas. Together they travelled to Italy and on return to Paris, Gandarillas financed a flat for Wood.

1922 Travelled through Europe, North Africa and Greece with Gandarillas. Wood moved in with Gandarillas.

1923 In March they travelled to the south of France and Italy. Returned to Paris end of May. Gandarillas' aunt Eugenia Errazuriz introduced Wood to Picasso, who gave him guidance and advice on his work.

1924 Wood travelled to Italy and on to the south of France in August. At the Hôtel Welcome in Villefranche, he met Jean Cocteau in October. On their return to Paris, Cocteau invited Wood to share his studio, an arrangement which lasted until the following February.

1925 Through Cocteau, Wood met Jean and Jeanne Bourgoint. In April, he journeyed to Marseilles, Monte Carlo where met Sergei Diaghilev, and Rome, again with Gandarillas. In September they returned to London, staying in Gandarillas' house at 14 Cheyne Walk, London. Wood took the top floor for a studio. Here, Wood worked on designs for Diaghilev's ballet, *Romeo and Juliet*.

1926 Returned to Villefranche in February. Back in Paris, Wood and Jeanne Bourgoint began a stormy relationship, which lasted until the following year. In

June, Wood travelled to London, where he met Ben and Winifred Nicholson and H.S. (Jim) Ede. He joined the 7&5 Society. In mid August, Wood and Gandarillas travelled to Cornwall, visiting the Isles of Scilly and Penzance before reaching St Ives in September. Wood stayed on alone in St Ives until the end of October.

1927 In January, Wood participated in his first exhibition with the 7&5 Society at the Beaux Arts Gallery, London. In April he exhibited again at the Beaux Arts Gallery with Ben and Winifred Nicholson and William Staite Murray. He met and had a brief but intense romance with Meraud Guiness in Monte Carlo. There was talk of marriage until her parents intervened and the relationship eventually fizzled out. In August, Wood travelled with Gandarillas and René Crevel to Vence in the south of France, where Crevel continued his convalescence from tuberculosis.

1928 Wood set up his own house at 234 King's Road, London. In February, Wood exhibited with the 7&5 Society at the Beaux Arts Gallery, and with Cedric Morris and Henri Gaudier-Brzeska at the Claridge Gallery, London. Wood spent six weeks during March and April at Bankshead, Ben and Winifred Nicholson's Cumberland home. Back in Paris, Wood met Frosca Munster, a married Russian expatriate, and they began an affair. He travelled back to Cornwall with the Nicholsons in July, staying at Foeck. Wood and Ben Nicholson visited St Ives, where they encountered Alfred Wallis. Wood stayed on alone in St Ives until late November in order to learn from Wallis. In December, he moved in with Munster in Paris.

1929 Wood set up house at 3 Minton Place, London. In April, he exhibited at Tooth's Gallery, London with Ben and Winifred Nicholson. He visited Dieppe with Munster and then travelled to Brittany in July. From August to October he stayed in Douarnenez and Tréboul, where he met Max Jacob at the Hôtel Ty-Mad.

1930 Wood journeyed again to Cornwall in March, staying at Mousehole, to prepare work for a solo exhibition in May at the Georges Bernheim Gallery, Paris. Worried he did not have enough work, he invited Ben Nicholson to share the show. Nicholson showed 10 works, while Wood showed over 25 paintings. The London dealer Lucy Wertheim bought 11 works by Wood. He returned to Tréboul in June, where he created more than 40 paintings in as many days. By late July, Wood was back in Paris, where he painted his most surealist works *Tiger and Arc de Triomphe* and *Zebra and Parachute* before leaving for England. On 21 August, Wood met his mother and sister for lunch. Later that day, witnesses saw him jump in front of a train at Salisbury Station.

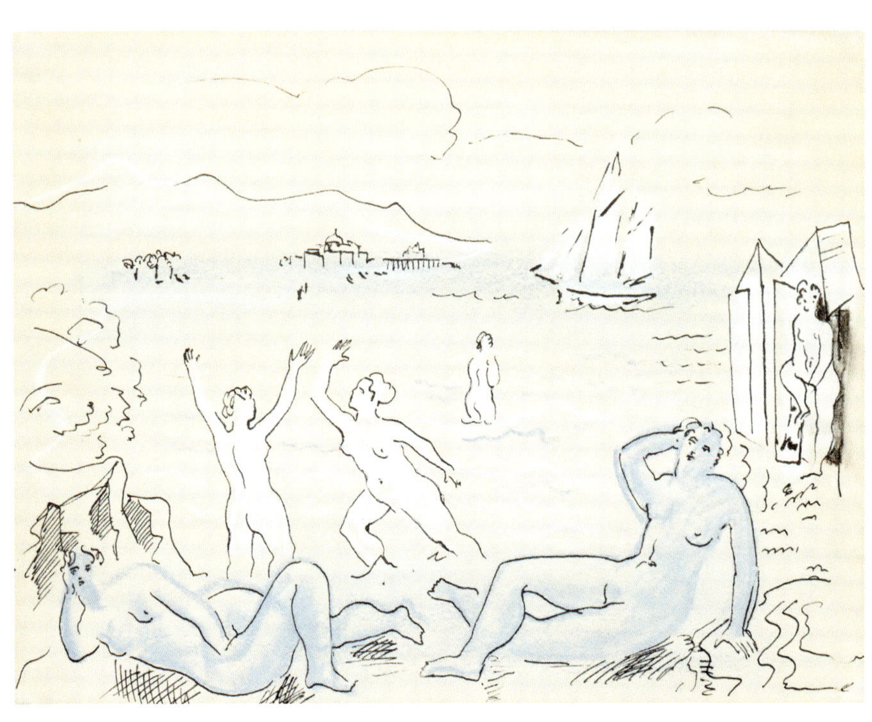

Brighton, undated. Ink and pastel on paper, 258 x 335 mm
Courtesy of the University of Essex

SELECTED EXHIBITIONS

* indicates publications

1927, January. Beaux Arts Gallery, London. 7&5 Society exhibition.

1927, April. Beaux Arts Gallery, London. 7&5 Society exhibition with Ben and Winifred Nicholson and William Staite Murray.

1928, February. Beaux Arts Gallery, London. 7&5 Society exhibition.

1928, February. Claridge Gallery, London. Exhibition of drawings by Christopher Wood, Cedric Morris and Henri Gaudier-Brzeska.

1929, April. Tooth & Sons Gallery, London with Ben and Winifred Nicholson.

1930, May. Georges Bernheim Gallery, Paris. 'Christopher Wood, Ben Nicholson: Deux Peintres Anglais' (Two English Painters).

1931, February. Wertheim Gallery, London. 'Exhibition of paintings by the late Christopher Wood'.

1932, April. Lefevre Gallery, London. 'Memorial Exhibition of the Most Recent Paintings by Christopher Wood'.*

1938, March. New Burlington Galleries arranged by the Redfern Gallery. 'Christopher Wood, Exhibition of Complete Works'.*

1938, June-October. British Pavillion, XX1 Venice Biennial.

1974, July-August. Kettle's Yard, Cambridge.*

1979, April. The Minories, Colchester.*

1989, October-November. Newlyn Art Gallery, Penzance. 'Christopher Wood: The Last Years 1928-1930'.*

1990, January-March. Kettle's Yard, Cambridge.*

1996, November-1997, April. Tate, St. Ives; **1997, May-August.** Musée des Beaux Arts, Quimper. 'Christopher Wood: A Painter Between Two Cornwalls'.*

2012, October-2013, June. Norwich Castle Museum, Mascalls Gallery, Kent, Falmouth Art Gallery. 'Cedric Morris and Christopher Wood: A Forgotten Friendship'.*

Further Reading:

Button, Virginia, *Christopher Wood*, London: Tate Publishing, 2003.

Faulks, Sebastian, *The Fatal Englishman: Three Short Lives*, London: Vintage, 1997.

Ingleby, Richard, *Christopher Wood: An English Painter*, London: Allison & Busby, 1995.

Newton, Eric, *Christopher Wood: His Life and Work*, London: Redfern Gallery, 1959.

Memoir of Christopher Wood entitled *'Kit'* by Jean Cocteau, date unknown
@ Tate, London 2013

Kit

à Max Jacob

Pour parler de peinture, hélas, je suis profane ;
Peut-être vaut-il mieux dire ce que je sais :
Entre autres que sa ville était le Londres d'Anne,
Lorsqu'elle faisait boire un grog chaud à Quincey.

Dans un monde où la mort ~~[illegible]~~ vivante nous taquine
Aimant les jeunes et les poètes beaucoup,
Il me faisait penser au prince Muichkine,
Souriant loin au lieu de rendre un mauvais coup.

Une énigme ~~chez~~ des l'ange est cette boiterie
Qu'il avait, ne posant sur terre que d'un pied.
Car son œuvre en exil attendait la patrie
Céleste, où nul ne vous demande vos papiers.

Jean Cocteau

☆

CHRISTOPHER WOOD

ISBN 978 1 904561 44 6

Published by Kettle's Yard,
University of Cambridge
Written and edited by
Elizabeth Fisher
Research by Jane Morgans
Design by paulallitt.com
Printed by C3 Imaging, Colchester
In an edition of 2500 copies

Christopher Wood
6 July - 1 September 2013
Kettle's Yard,
University of Cambridge

Curated by Elizabeth Fisher
Assisted by Jane Morgans

With thanks to
Elisabeth Swan, Mary Adams,
Richard Ingleby, Anne Goodchild,
Anthony Hepworth, Guy Haywood,
Claire Daunton, Louise Marks and
Kath Wood.

Kettle's Yard
Castle Street, Cambridge CB3 0AQ
United Kingdom
+44(0)1223 748100
www.kettlesyard.co.uk

Director: Andrew Nairne
Chair: Anne Lonsdale

IMAGE CREDITS

pp.. 2, 4, 28, 37, 43, 46, 48, 50,
63, 69, 77, 79, 80; courtesy
Public Catalogue Foundation
pp.. 32, 33, 34, 35, 53, 56, 59,
64, 70; Peter Mennim
pp.. 16, 18, 21, 23; Paul Allitt
p. 58; Anthony Hepworth
inside cover; © estate of
Ben Nicholson/Tate, London 2010
pp.. 60, 95; © Tate, London 2013

cover:
Le Phare (detail) *see* p. 77

right:
Christopher Wood monogram
on a shirt kept by Jim Ede

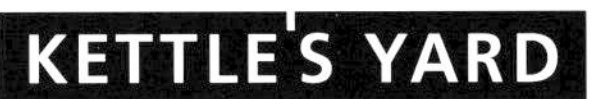

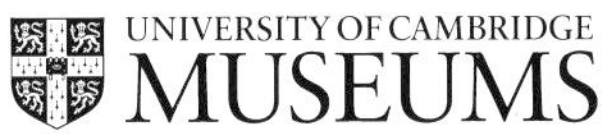

SUPPORTING KETTLE'S YARD

Kettle's Yard relies on the generosity of supporters to care for the collection and historic buildings, and enable us to offer a full programme of activities, from exhibitions, education activities and music to publications and research. All gifts, large and small, help to safeguard the collection for future generations, and enable others to enjoy Kettle's Yard now and in the future.

There are a variety of ways in which you can help support Kettle's Yard and also benefit as a UK or US taxpayer. For more information please visit **www.kettlesyard.co.uk/supporters**

KETTLE'S YARD RECEIVES
REGULAR FUNDING FROM:

Arts Council England
Cambridge City Council
The Higher Education Funding Council
The Friends of Kettle's Yard
and many other individual donors

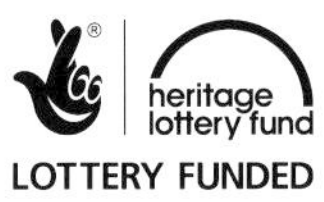

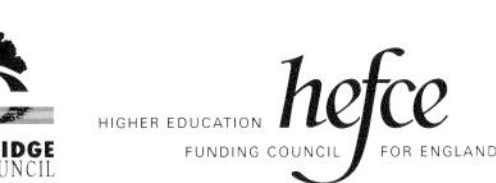

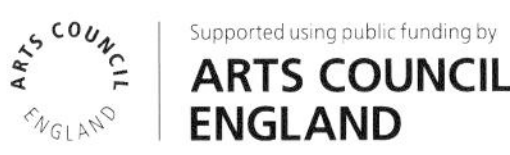